7

Bow Church.

Cheap Croff

S Laurens   Guill

Cole harbour

Gally fuste

The Globe

SHAKESPEARE
the Elizabethan

Martin Droeshout sculpsit London.

To the Reader.

This Figure, that thou here seest put,
 It was for gentle Shakespeare cut;
Wherein the Grauer had a strife
 with Nature, to out-doo the life:
O, could he but haue drawne his wit
 As well in brasse, as he hath hit
Hisface; the Print would then surpasse
 All, that was euer writ in brasse.
But, since he cannot, Reader, looke
 Not on his Picture, but his Booke.
        B. I.

SHAKESPEARE
the Elizabethan

A. L. Rowse

*New intellectual truth does not triumph by
convincing its opponents and making them
see the light; but rather because its
opponents eventually die, and a
new generation grows up that
is familiar with it.*
MAX PLANCK

G. P. Putnam's Sons
NEW YORK

COPY 1

Designed by Tim Higgins
for George Weidenfeld and Nicolson Ltd.,
11 St John's Hill, London SW11

SBN: 399-11889-6
Library of Congress Catalog Card Number: 76-44575

Printed in England

TO

GERALD EADES BENTLEY

our leading authority on
the Jacobean Drama

❧ Contents ❧

I

Stratford Beginnings

THE SHAKESPEAREAN DRAMA is the undying glory of the Elizabethan age, and no writer was ever more a man of the theatre than William Shakespeare. Beginning as a player, he went on to become the most successful playwright of the age. A sharer in the Lord Chamberlain's Company from its formation in 1594, he was one of the inner core of Fellows – with Burbage, Heming and Condell, to whom Shakespeare left remembrances in his will, while the last two brought out his plays as a tribute to his memory – who made the Company the premier in London, recognized as such (the King's Men) on James I's accession in 1603. Shakespeare took his share in the business of the Company, occasionally receiving the money for performances and, no doubt, producing. He ended up as part-owner of the Blackfriars theatre, and an independent gentleman in his native town of Stratford, a status achieved by his winnings from his life of hard and inspired work.

The drama was closely connected with the scholastic profession, both at school and university. Plays were frequently performed at both, often written and produced by such famous schoolmasters as Nicholas Udall of Eton and Westminster, Richard Mulcaster of Merchant Taylors, Thomas Ashton of Shrewsbury, Richard Edwards and George Peele of Christ Church, Oxford. We learn from a son of a colleague of Shakespeare that he was 'in his younger years a schoolmaster in the country'. This is corroborated by the way in which grammar school education is to the fore in his work, while his earliest plays in both comedy and tragedy are much influenced by the texts chiefly used in Elizabethan schools, Plautus and Seneca.

Shakespeare's life, 1564–1616, is roughly coterminous with the Elizabethan age itself, for its impetus and some of its leading figures went on well into James's reign. (Robert Cecil, Earl of Salisbury, really ran the country until his death in 1612.)

William Shakespeare was baptized on 26 April 1564 – the usual custom then was a few days after birth – in the parish church of Holy Trinity at

OPPOSITE ABOVE Shakespeare's birthplace at Stratford before it was restored
OPPOSITE BELOW The upper chamber in Shakespeare's birthplace at Stratford

9

Stratford Beginnings

The font at Stratford in which Shakespeare was baptized

Stratford-upon-Avon, where he was buried fifty-two years later, having died on 23 April 1616. He was the eldest son of John Shakespeare and Mary Arden, who had come into the busy market town from Arden country, the wooded countryside to the north of it. Mary Arden was something of an heiress, out at Wilmcote, of good family. The Arden side of his inheritance may have meant more to William Shakespeare, with his emphasis on gentility and the record of his life very much in keeping. When established securely with the success of the Lord Chamberlain's Company, and beginning to prosper, in 1596 he took out a coat-of-arms in his father's name; shortly after there was a proposal to quarter it with the arms of Arden, gentle-folk of the northern part of the county.

John Shakespeare's marriage enabled him to play a prominent part in the town's affairs for some twenty years, ending up as bailiff, or mayor, of the borough. He evidently devoted too much time to them; from 1577, his own affairs became involved and burdened with debt. At this time his clever, observant son would be a schoolboy of thirteen at the grammar school. He did not go on to university, unlike his rival and contemporary, Christopher Marlowe; but a recognizable grammar school education, with its devotion to Ovid, its tags from textbooks, Bible and Prayer Book, provided a sufficient foundation for his subsequent development. Most people's education takes place after schooldays, and a man of genius educates himself.

No less important than grammar school in the boy's formation was regular attendance at church, either in the parish church or the Guild Chapel next to the school – where it fell to John Shakespeare, as chamberlain of the borough, in the year before his son's birth, to whitewash the Last Judgment over the chancel arch which we see uncovered today. Elizabethans had by law to attend church regularly. From earliest childhood there were services – morning and evening prayer, communion at intervals, catechizing, sermons, teaching, saying the prayers, singing the psalms. Of all Shakespeare's 'sources' this is the one most constantly reflected, from first to last; and, above all, the Psalms in their Prayer Book version, for this is what he heard in church all his life: there is not a play of his that does not reflect a phrase or suggestion. There are allusions from almost all the books of the Bible: in the earlier half of his work from the Bishops' Bible used in church; in the later, more often from the Genevan version he evidently possessed.

The family lived in a house in Henley Street, at the elmy end of the town; here John Shakespeare had his glover's shop, and his stall on market days at the crossways at the upper end of Bridge Street. William was well acquainted with every variety of skin, and their different uses, and refers familiarly to the glover's paring-knife. His brothers and sisters were christened in the parish church; his bachelor brother Gilbert took possession of the land his successful brother bought, when William was too busy to do so himself; and a youngest brother Edmund followed him into the theatre to become a player. Edmund died at twenty-seven and was buried in St Mary Overy, now Southwark Cathedral, hard by the Globe Theatre. Sister Joan married one Hart, a hatter, and her family continued at Stratford into the eighteenth century. William left them bequests in his will, including the old family

ABOVE Shakespeare's
grammar school
at Stratford

LEFT A school in
Shakespeare's time

Sir Thomas Lucy's Charlecote

home for her life. Her grandson, Charles Hart, bred up at Blackfriars as a boy-player, became a leading actor at the Restoration.

William Shakespeare refers to his 'sportive blood', and it is evident that he was an active-bodied, out-of-doors countryman – unlike the more academic Marlowe, denizen of Canterbury and Cambridge. Shakespeare was addicted to all forms of sport; the gentlemanly game of bowls is much to the fore in his imagery, while we can see him at the more demotic practice of archery – the butts at Stratford were on the level ground by the river between the present theatre and the bridge so familiar to him:

> In my schooldays, when I had lost one shaft,
> I shot his fellow of the self-same flight
> The self-same way, with more advisèd watch,
> To find the other forth; and by adventuring both
> I oft found both.   [*The Merchant of Venice*, 1.i.140]

Naturally and convincingly, country sports are much more in the foreground in his early work when he was still a young man. Out on the stubbles on the high ground north of the town there was coursing the hare; and *Venus and Adonis* has a long inset – nothing to do with the story –

The Hare, to the Hunter

ARe mindes of men, become fo voyde of fenfe,
That they can ioye to hurte a harmeleffe thing?
A fillie beaft, whiche cannot make defence?
A wretche? a worme that can not bite, nor fting?
If that be fo, I thanke my Maker than,
For makyng me, a Beaft and not a Man.

Coursing the hare

describing hare coursing. Most of all, the early writings reveal a regular fixation on hunting or poaching deer – very popular with young sparks at the time, with students at the universities, and such. This seems to have got him into not very serious trouble with Sir Thomas Lucy, the local magnate out at Charlecote. It did not, however, prevent him from mentioning Lucy's ancestor in friendly fashion in his early play, *Henry VI*, while a pun on the family coat-of-arms provided him with a joke later in *The Merry Wives of Windsor*.

A more weighty outcome of his high spirits was his getting Anne Hathaway with child at the age of eighteen, when she was eight and a half years older – getting on for an Elizabethan spinster. The Hathaways were good yeomen folk out at Shottery; William being a minor and Anne's father dead, a special marriage licence was necessary in November 1582. It was usual enough, then as now, to anticipate the pleasures of the marriage bed – but in those days far more frequent for the girl to go pregnant to her wedding. Nor did her condition detract from the youthful bridegroom's enthusiasm:

> O let me clip ye [embrace]
> In arms as sound as when I wooed, in heart
> As merry as when our nuptial day was done
> And tapers burned to bedward!
> [*Coriolanus*, I.vi.31]

We can see them still in the old house in Henley Street, which they shared with his parents in the way Elizabethans did, great and small. Six months after the special licence, in May 1583 their eldest child, Susanna, was born. Susanna was not a Shakespeare or Arden family name: it bespeaks the youthful father's humorous imagination, with its suggestion of the peeping elders – a favourite theme for Elizabethan depiction. This eldest child was the one who took after her father. Twenty months later, in February 1585, twins followed: Hamnet and Judith, named for the godparents, neighbours Hamnet and Judith Sadler, who in turn called their son William. No more children were born to Anne Shakespeare, now a woman of thirty.

Stratford was a tightly knit, neighbourly community, a busy market town with good communications into the midlands and Wales, down the Severn or over Clopton's fine bridge to Oxford and London. John Shakespeare, who dealt considerably in wool, had business dealings with the father of Richard Field, who took the high road to London before William. Richard Field married the widow of a well-known printer, Vautrollier, and succeeded to the business in Blackfriars, where he printed his fellow Stratford lad's poems, *Venus and Adonis* and *The Rape of Lucrece*.

At twenty-one, in 1585, William had a wife and three children to support. Christopher Marlowe, determinedly homosexual, had no such encumbrances and, on leaving Cambridge, had an immediate success with his *Tamburlane*. John Shakespeare's affairs were going downhill; he was in debt and having to sell off his wife's property, including her inheritance out at Wilmcote to her sister's family, the Lamberts. In 1587 William had to join with his father in mortgaging it; though later, when he had recouped the family fortunes and tried to recover it, they never got it back.

The professional troupes of players, which became such a feature of the Elizabethan age, began to visit Stratford as early as 1569. But there were already Christmas mummings and Whitsun pastorals in which likely lads were sure to have a part — as he describes in one of his early plays, where so much of his youthful background is depicted, called upon for material before life gathered thickening and deepening experience:

> At Pentecost, [Whitsun]
> When all our pageants of delight were played,
> Our youth got me to play the woman's part,
> And I was trimmed in Madam Julia's gown,
> Which servèd me as fit, by all men's judgments,
> As if the garment had been made for me.
> [*The Two Gentlemen of Verona*, IV.iv.163]

This discouraging year, 1587, saw the largest number of professional troupes visiting the town. When the foremost among them, the Queen's Company, reached Stratford it was wanting a player, for one of them had been killed by another actor on the road. The slain man's widow married John Heming, who was to become one of Shakespeare's closest colleagues.

Soon William was taking the road to London, following in the footsteps of Richard Field.

2

Shakespeare and his Patron, Southampton

THE EXCITING YEARS just before and after the Armada of 1588 saw the leap forward of the theatre into literature, largely the work of Christopher Marlowe, closely followed by William Shakespeare – to be followed again a decade later by Ben Jonson. The astonishing output of plays was really the work of the professionals; Marlowe and Jonson were not strictly professionals but literary men writing plays among other things – to be a poet was the great thing in that age, offering superior standing to a playwright. Shakespeare was a professional to his fingertips: first and foremost an actor, and a good one (unlike Ben), who took to writing plays and then challenged fame as a poet and got himself recognized.

By 1592 he was recognized all right as a successful, coming man and, in the usual way, by an envious rival, Robert Greene. Greene was a university wit, a Cambridge man, the leading denizen of literary Bohemia, well acquainted with low life; an excellent prose writer and novelist, he was less successful with his plays, which he had been reduced to writing at the behest of the players. This was what embittered him, for he was being outclassed by one of them he knew, a junior, nine years younger, a mere actor, no university man, who thought himself as good a poet as the best of them and was ready to turn his hand to anything.

Greene was on his deathbed when he wrote his notorious attack, warning his Cambridge fellows, Marlowe and Nash, against the strenuous competition of this outsider – that was the sting in it – the newcomer 'beautified with our feathers'; there follows a gibe at a resounding line from the third part of *Henry VI*, with which the newcomer had achieved popular success. It is clear that there had been some contact between the player and the writer to account for the latter's venom. For Greene depicts a euphoric player, well pleased with himself, up from the country with a provincial accent, who dressed like a gentleman and claimed to be one. The world had once gone hard with him touring about the country, where for seven years he had been

Shakespeare dedicated *Venus and Adonis* to his patron, young Southampton

TO THE RIGHT
HONOVRABLE, HENRY
VVriothesley, Earle of Southhampton,
and Baron of Titchfield.

THE loue I dedicate to your Lordſhip is without end: wherof this Pamphlet without beginning is but a ſuperfluous Moity. The warrant I haue of your Honourable diſpoſition, not the worth of my vntutord Lines makes it aſſured of acceptance. VVhat I haue done is yours, what I haue to doe is yours, being part in all I haue, deuoted yours. VVere my worth greater, my duety would ſhew greater, meane time, as it is, it is bound to your Lordſhip; To whom I wiſh long life ſtill lengthned with all happineſſe.

Your Lordſhips in all duety.

William Shakeſpeare.

A 2

Enter Tamora pleadinge for her sonnes
goinge to execution

Tam: Stay Romane bretheren gratious Conquerors
Victorious Titus rue the teares I shed
A mothers teares in passion of her sonnes
And if thy sonnes weere euer deare to thee
Oh, thinke my sonnes to bee as deare to mee
Sufficeth, not that wee are brought to Roome
To beautifye thy triumphes and returne
Captiue to thee and to thy Romane yoake
But must my sonnes be slaughtered in the streetes
for valiant doynges in there Cuntryes cause
Oh, if to fight for kinge and Common weale
Weare pietye in thine it is in these
Andronicus staine not thy tombe wth blood
Wilt thou drawe neere the nature of the Gods
drawe neere them then in beinge mercifull
Sweete mercy is nobilityes true badge
Thrice noble Titus spare my first borne sonne

Titus   Patient your sellf madame for by hee must
Anon do you likewise prepare your sellf
Chiron   And now at last repent your wicked liffe
Ay now I curse the day and yet I thinke
few comes wthin the compasse of my curse
wherein I did not some notorious ill
As kill a man or els deuise his death
Rauish a mayd or plott the way to do it
Accuse some innocent and forsweare my sellf
Sett deadly enmity betweene too freendes
Make poore mens cattell breake there neckes
Sett fire on barnes and haystalkes in the night
And bid the owners quench them wth there teares
Oft haue I digd vp dead men from there graues
... ...

'an absolute interpreter of the puppets'. Interestingly enough, it was just seven years since the birth of his twins in 1585 had forced Shakespeare to look further afield to support his young family. Now, well set up, he was able to offer Greene a job penning plays and lodge him 'at the town's end in a house of retail'.

That was what actors could now do for writers, university men, to whom they were beholden for their plays and yet would forsake in their necessity – the necessity Greene was in, dying in hardship and debt, attended by a strumpet, sister of a hanged cut-purse. He held up his fate as a bitter warning to Marlowe and Nash – who in the event did not much better.

Shakespeare much resented the attack, and called on Chettle, who had published it and evidently had not yet met him, to apologize. He indited the handsomest apology I know of in that age, having now 'seen his demeanour no less civil than he excellent in the quality he professes', in other words his bearing no less gentlemanly than he was accomplished as an actor. Besides that, 'divers of worship' had spoken up for him; that is, upper-class folk or eminent citizens, who had testified to 'his uprightness of dealing', which showed him an honourable man, as his easy grace in writing showed his mastery of his art.

We may complete this testimony to his character by what Ben Jonson, who was in the best position to know, said of him later: 'He was indeed honest [i.e. honourable], and of an open and free nature.'

What tributes these were, how consistent and revealing! The age called him 'gentle': that meant, at that time, gentlemanly; it was a very important side to him – and he was one of the few among the theatre folk to behave like a gentleman. This was a great advantage to him in gaining access to upper-class society, where he was able to enjoy complete independence of spirit (Ben Jonson had to assert it) and conduct himself with easy grace of manner.

What won him the applause of the wide public was a play on the theme of the Hundred Years' War with France – always popular, it brought back memories of Agincourt and Crécy, Henry the hero–king and brave, fighting Talbot. Nash bears witness to the public response to seeing Talbot brought alive on the stage again, greeted with the tears of thousands of spectators – the audience were much more involved with the action then; for the stage jutted out among them, and the action was beheld almost in the round. The actor–dramatist's play on this theme was so successful that he had to write a sequel, and yet another: the three parts of *Henry VI*. Greene had reason to be envious.

It was the Normandy campaign of 1591, under the darling hero of the Elizabethan populace, Essex, that stirred up these memories and brought them to the surface. We still sing that stout tune of the Hundred Years' War, 'Our King went forth to Normandy'; on D-Day, 1944, a young commander was reciting Henry v's speech before Agincourt, from Shakespeare's *Henry V*, as his landing-craft neared the coast of Normandy.

The expedition to France, the opening up of the war on land, was being prepared in 1590–1. Essex's glamour appealed to the young gallants of the time, and early in 1591 the Earl of Southampton, only seventeen and keen to win honour and renown in action, slipped across the Channel, without

A scene from *Titus Andronicus*

permission of the Queen or the Lord Treasurer, his guardian, to offer himself to Essex's service. The young Earl was also keen to win regard as a patron of the arts; books were increasingly dedicated to him, he was often painted – for the youth was beautiful in a rather feminine way (which the Renaissance admired), and poets sought his patronage, since he was well educated, a friend to letters and an addict of plays. Again one does not have to look far for what drew this generous young peer to the successful dramatist of the *Henry VI* plays.

By this time the actor had not only written these chronicle – plays, with their bloodstained action, but the even bloodier *Titus Andronicus*; his comic spirit expressed itself in *The Comedy of Errors* and *The Two Gentlemen of Verona*. And shortly, in even more authentic vein, came *The Taming of the Shrew* with its references to Warwickshire and redolent of the Cotswolds. This play begins with a rather nostalgic Induction calling up the scenes and evocations of his youth. It includes a return from hunting and a good deal of knowledgeable talk about hounds, Christopher Sly is Old Sly's son of Barton-on-the-Heath, where Shakespeare's Arden aunt, Joan Lambert, lived. We have Marion Hacket, the 'fat ale-wife of Wincot', near Stratford, and

> Stephen Sly and old John Naps of Greet –
> [*The Taming of the Shrew*, Induction, ii.95]

not far away. At the end, the players who are to perform the play proper arrive, and are taken to the buttery to be given meat and drink. It must often have happened just like that to Shakespeare as a player: to be shown into the buttery, like a servant.

He was more anxious to shine as a poet – his sheer literary ambition has never been sufficiently emphasized (though it had been realized well enough by Greene). He seized his opportunity to address to young Southampton his prentice piece, *A Lover's Complaint*, in which the ambivalent youth is recognizably described along with his popularity:

> That he did in the general bosom reign
> Of young, of old; and sexes both enchanted.
> [*A Lover's Complaint*, 127]

He certainly came to enchant William.

He was born Henry Wriothesley – pronounced Risley – on 6 October 1573, and so was nine and a half years younger than Shakespeare. His father had died young:

> Dear my love, you know
> You had a father: let your son say so.
> [*Sonnets*, XIII]

It was essential that the young heir should marry and do his duty by the family – all the more so since they were somewhat exposed by being Catholics. He had been brought up as a ward of Lord Treasurer Burghley, head of the Cecil family, who saw to it that he was well educated at Cambridge and got a promise that the youth would marry his grand-daughter, the talented, wayward, half-crazy Oxford's daughter. As he approached his majority everybody was anxious to see him safely married:

Southampton at the time of the *Sonnets*

Queen Elizabeth I at a deer hunt

his grandfather, Lord Montagu, the great Lord Burghley, not least his charming mother, the Countess:

> Thou art thy mother's glass, and she in thee
> Calls back the lovely April of her prime.
>
> [*Sonnets*, III]

It is the theme with which Shakespeare's sonnets to his patron began, nor would it be disagreeable to his anxious mother. (Their dedication years later, after her death, to 'Mr W.H.' was not Shakespeare's, but the publisher's.)

That Shakespeare won Southampton's patronage at this moment was a great stroke of fortune – Nash, who tried to recommend himself, was rejected – for 1592 was a bad plague year, followed by yet another. This was disastrous to the theatre people, for the theatres in London were mostly closed for two years in succession. Companies took to the roads, were broken or merged with others; the family of one leading actor was wiped out, and we know the dangers and precautions taken by Edward Alleyn and his wife's stepfather, Henslowe, the theatrical entrepreneur, from their

21

VIVETIE·VT·SOLITVS·VIVB·DIV·VT·MERITVS

Queen Elizabeth's
Lord Treasurer Burghley

surviving correspondence. Something of these black years is reflected in the deaths of writers for the theatre. In 1592 Greene died, and so did Thomas Watson, the admired Latin poet and translator of Italian madrigals; in 1593 his friend Marlowe was killed in the notorious tavern brawl at Deptford; that winter he was followed by Thomas Kyd, the leading tragedian with his famous *Spanish Tragedy* and, not long after, by the versatile George Peele.

We note the increasing urgency as the sonnets proceed:

> And life no longer than thy love will stay,
> For it depends upon that love of thine. . . .
> [*Sonnets*, XCII]

At first all was set fair in the relationship with the golden youth. From the beginning Shakespeare makes it clear that he was not interested in him sexually; we do not know what the young man's attitude was, though we know that he was ambivalent, not yet sexually directed.

> And for a woman wert thou first created;
> Till Nature, as she wrought thee, fell a-doting,
> And, by addition, me of thee defeated
> By adding one thing to my purpose nothing.
>
> [*Sonnets*, XX]

And as if it were not sufficiently clear to what Shakespeare is referring, he makes it doubly so with a characteristic piece of bawdy:

> But since she pricked thee out for women's pleasure,
> Mine be thy love, and thy love's use their treasure.
>
> [*Sonnets*, XX]

On the other hand, Southampton may have found Shakespeare's virility attractive in itself, for the player was highly sexed but heterosexual, more than normally responsive where women were concerned. Shakespeare would have been only too happy, he says, if the youth had been a girl; but in their lives there was a 'separable spite', not only in sex and age, but rank and conditions, the exigencies of their lives, the very differing demands upon them.

Shakespeare had reason to be intensely grateful, not only for a measure of support during these difficult years – the sonnets show him jogging along on his horse into the country, to which he regularly retreated in summer – but for his introduction to a cultivated society, such as his nature yearned for and to which it responded with alacrity and enthusiasm. It has been noticed in his imagery how his senses became sharpened and refined. Before, there was a varied talent and beckoning promise in his productions; henceforward there is unmistakable genius: it is the difference between *Henry VI* and *Richard II*, between *The Comedy of Errors* and *A Midsummer Night's Dream*. There was not only a new world opening out before him with its opportunities, but a new world of experience – of friendship with a talented and responsive youth, a star in the Elizabethan firmament; then of infatuation for a sophisticated woman, of questionable but strong and challenging personality, with a courtly background. Above all, for a writer, there was a new inspiration for his work: a poet is in love with the idea of being in love.

The effects of it all, of these crucial, decisive three years in his life – when he was twenty-eight, twenty-nine, thirty, no longer young for an Elizabethan – begin to be seen at once in his work. Intermission from playing in the public theatres gave him the time to write his two long poems, with which he challenged fame as a poet. Moreover, acceptance by the young Earl as his poet, in the regular Elizabethan fashion, meant addressing his work to him, as he proceeded to do – not only his sonnets, which are verse-letters to the patron, but the two plays which relate to the circle, *Love's Labour's Lost* and *A Midsummer Night's Dream*:

> Since all alike my songs and praises be
> To one, of one, still such, and ever so –
>
> [*Sonnets*, CV]

There was no other. This means clearly that both his songs, i.e. the poems, and the sonnets in praise of his patron – they are full of his praises – are alike devoted to him alone. The poems were publicly dedicated to him; and the sonnets were no less written for him. The very word 'praises' occurs frequently in the *Sonnets*; understandably and corroboratively, since they are written for the patron.

The address, or *envoi*, at the end of the first twenty-six sonnets – mainly concerned with the theme of the young Earl's duty to marry, carry on the family, and duplicate his own beauty – dedicates them to the patron:

> Lord of my love, to whom in vassalage
> Thy merit hath my *duty* strongly knit,
> To thee I send this written ambassage
> To witness *duty*, not to show my wit:
> *Duty* so great.... [*Sonnets*, XXVI]

It is the language, deferential yet dignified, with which the poet publicly dedicated his first long poem, *Venus and Adonis*, to his patron in the next year, 1593. He promises to present him with some 'graver labour' later, 'Your Honour's in all *duty*, William Shakespeare'. The poem was printed by his Stratford acquaintance, Richard Field, from his shop in Blackfriars.

The theme of the poem reflects – and Shakespeare was a great one for seizing the moment, in his plays too throughout his career – his patron's recognizable situation: he would not respond to women's love, any more than the provokingly handsome Adonis would to Venus, who reproaches him:

> Art thou a woman's son and canst not feel
> What 'tis to love? [*Venus and Adonis*, 201]

The poem was something new, with this quite different turn, scintillating and fresh, naughty and distinctly stimulating. It was immediately successful, and appealed to the new kind of audience Shakespeare – with his ambition, literary and social – could have hoped for: the Court and fashionable young men at the Inns of Court and the universities. It went into many editions.

Next year, 1594, he fulfilled his promise to his patron with a graver poem, *The Rape of Lucrece*, also printed by Field. This was a very different affair, as befitted a sombre subject; the atmosphere is altogether heavier, guilt-laden, weighed down by the obsession with sex, self-questioning, the reproaches of conscience, remorse; perhaps most significant, the conflict between clear reason and the infatuation of lust:

> What win I, if I gain the thing I seek?
> A dream, a breath, a froth of fleeting joy.
> [*The Rape of Lucrece*, 212]

The poem had less popular success, but was more appreciated by the graver sort, like Gabriel Harvey at Cambridge. Its dedication to Southampton is notable for its charged, emotional language: 'the love I dedicate to your lordship is without end.... What I have done is yours, what I have to do is yours, being part of all I have, devoted yours ... Your Lordship's in all *duty*, William Shakespeare'.

Southampton's mother, whose second marriage was to Vice-Chamberlain Heneage, and third to Sir William Harvey

ÆTATIS. 13. 1565
THE EARLE OF
SOVTE HAMPTON

A great deal had happened in those three years to account for this unique dedication, with its implications and all that lies behind it. The whole story is uniquely revealed in the sonnets, much too near the bone, much too autobiographical an exposure to be published as a whole. They were never published by Shakespeare, but laid by in the Southampton *cache*, until years later the publisher Thorpe in 1609 produced them, all too grateful to the one person who had got the manuscript: someone in the Southampton circle, Mr W.H. Some of the sonnets – the earlier were harmless enough – were passed round in the circle; but when some of them were printed without permission, by William Jaggard, Thomas Heywood – a fellow dramatist –

The *Sonnets*: first edition

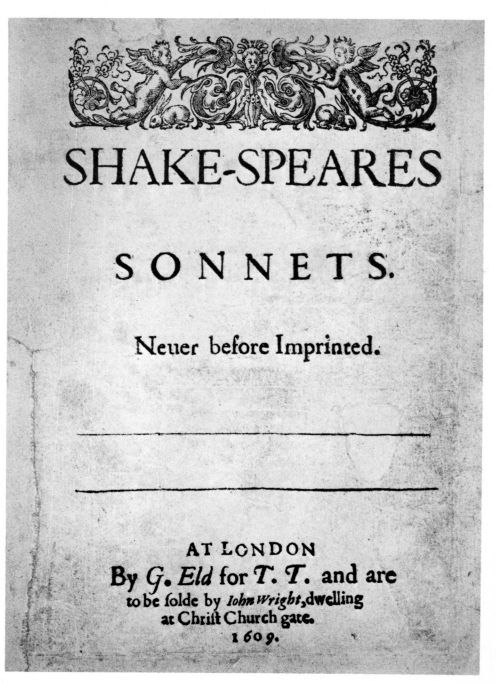

SHAKE-SPEARES

SONNETS.

Neuer before Imprinted.

AT LONDON
By *G. Eld* for *T. T.* and are
to be folde by *Iohn Wright*, dwelling
at Chrift Church gate.
1609.

tells us that 'the author, as I know, was much offended thereat'. And, considering what was in many of them, no wonder!

For it is a complex, intricate, unique story that is revealed: every light and shadow upon friendship, expectation, ecstasy, disillusionment; the complications and dissatisfactions of intense, intimate relationships; the happiness and sadness incident to all affairs of the heart; the rivalries, the treacheries when others come in to darken innocence; obsession, regret, remorse, driving the sensitive soul to the edge of madness. Everything is in the sonnets, read as a whole; few have done so with enough knowledge of the background to interpret what is being said. Yet Shakespeare's nature was candid, 'open and free'; he does in fact tell us everything. Here we can give only a brief outline of what he reveals to us from the heart.

The dates of these happenings are quite precise and they are determining; they are in intelligible sequence, but they need an historian to read them from the topical references. For want of that, all has been unclear in the past, and confusion has prevailed.

> Three winters cold
> Have from the forests shook three summers' pride –

that is, the winters of 1591–2, 1592–3, and 1593–4 –

> Three beauteous springs to yellow autumn turned . . .
> Since first I saw you fresh.   [*Sonnets*, CIV]

The acquaintance actually began in the winter of 1591–2. Early on in the paradisal relationship of the poet with his generous and golden-natured patron, a woman comes between. Shakespeare was to blame, as we might expect. She was a lady of superior social standing, so, in usual Elizabethan fashion, he got the young lord to write to her on behalf of his poet. The lady uses the opportunity to entangle the youth, a better proposition altogether than an impecunious player–poet. This development gives Shakespeare anxiety, for he has a feeling of responsibility for the fatherless young peer, in addition to affection and gratitude; he does not know what is happening between them, but he has reason to fear and deplore the fact, if it is so, that this, instead of married happiness, should be the youth's introduction to sexual experience with women. Evidently the lady is not a desirable acquaintance for the innocent, unmarried youth – though all too desirable for the highly sexed, heterosexual Shakespeare.

A Certaine man longed to see A gentle woman whom he loued
& desired to halk to· and becaus he could not tell howe to com to
her & wher he should be welcom to her or noe, Moued this question
whether yt were best to send to her to knowe howe she did· And
therbi to hi whon she wold bid the messenger bid his mr com
to her or not· Thinkinge therby that he might gather therby
to see her· 1597 the 11 Septemb ☉ p m at on· et quid incidit de ea·
James·

Best to somewhat lang dels harborne
1597 20 Septemb at p m 30 p 5·

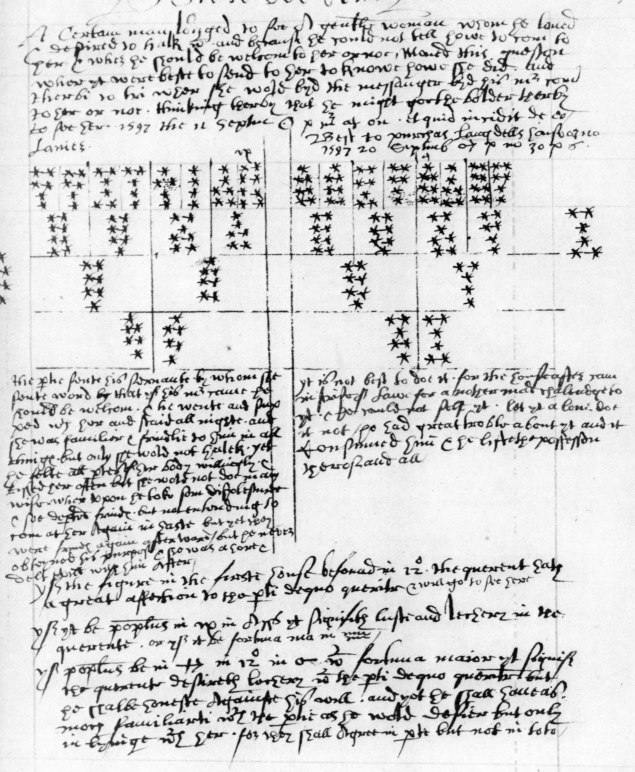

3

The Rival Poet; and the Dark Lady

SHORTLY AFTERWARDS, a further complication appears: a rival poet, who offers a real challenge, a danger to Shakespeare's possession of the young man's affections. What is he rivalling Shakespeare for, but the patronage of the patron? Nash offered no threat; what makes this newcomer dangerous is that he is superior to Shakespeare, both as a poet and in learning – an intellectual. He is that 'able spirit', that 'worthier pen'; he is a ship 'of tall building and of goodly pride . . . of the proudest sail', while Shakespeare's is but 'a saucy boat . . . worthless, if he thrive and I be cast away'. The rival writes 'with golden quill', 'in polished form', with precious phrases refined by all the muses.

Shakespeare had reason to fear such a rival, especially now, in 1593, with plague continuing and theatres closed again. Then, quite suddenly, the rival disappears; after several sonnets about him, all in the present tense – half a dozen or so, since the rivalry occupied only a short space of time – the affair concludes with a powerful valedictory sonnet, all in the past tense. The rival is not mentioned again; but he is very recognizable from Shakespeare's description, beginning:

> Was it the proud full sail of his great verse?

Marlowe was famous for his powerful blank verse – 'Marlowe's mighty line', in Ben Jonson's phrase.

> Was it his spirit, by spirits taught to write
> Above a mortal pitch, that struck me dead?
> [*Sonnets*, LXXXVI]

Marlowe knew all about trafficking with the spirits, as we know from the formulae for summoning them up in *Dr Faustus*; and the sonnet further refers to Mephistophilis in the play, that nightly gulls Faustus with intelligence, enticing him on.

Marlowe was killed in the inn at Deptford on 30 May 1593, aged twenty-

Forman visits the Dark Lady

29

Lord, haue mercy

on London.

I follow.

We fly.

Wee dye.

Keepe out

The plague in London

nine: the greatest loss our literature ever suffered. There is no knowing what he might have accomplished. But his death removed the greatest rival to Shakespeare – and the chief influence upon him – from the scene. At the time of his death he was writing *Hero and Leander* in competition with Shakespeare's *Venus and Adonis* for Southampton's favour. We do not know what would have happened if Marlowe had lived and completed it; for, even though unfinished, it is superior as a work of art to Shakespeare's poem.

The inspirer of it is recognizably the same, and there are many parallel phrases:

> Some swore he was a maid in man's attire,
> For in his looks were all that men desire . . .
> Why art thou not in love – and loved of all?[1]

His 'dangling tresses' are very familiar in Southampton's early portraits – no Greek Leander; and Marlowe begins his poem with a graceful salute to the rival theme of Venus and Adonis. Now he was dead.

The dubious embroilment with the equivocal lady, and the tension of the rivalry with a famous poet – who enjoyed the lead with his plays, so long as he lived – imposed a double strain upon the relations between the poet and his young patron. Innocence had vanished, and with it security of heart

[1] Marlowe, *Hero and Leander*, l.83 foll.

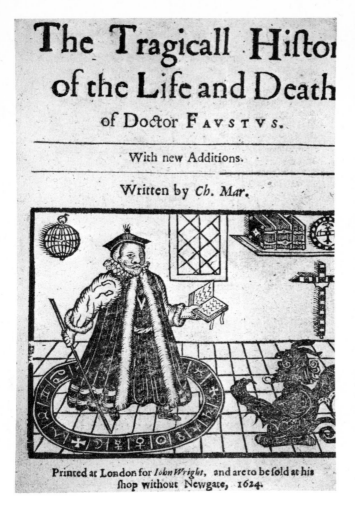

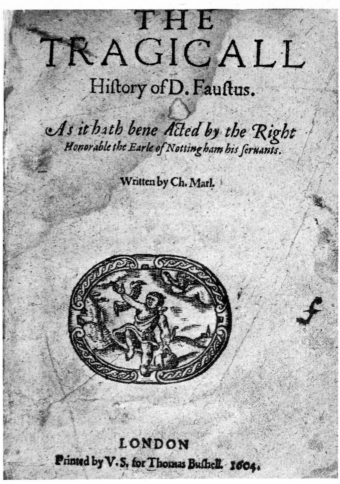

Marlowe's most famous play

and mind; but Shakespeare is dependent on his lord, and is in a rather humiliating position in acknowledging:

> I do forgive thy robbery, gentle thief,
> Although thou steal thee all my poverty.
>
> [*Sonnets*, XL]

Then, with a generous return:

> Take all my loves, my love, yea, take them all:
> What hast thou then more than thou hadst before?
>
> [*Sonnets*, XL]

This is followed by an access of reproach:

> Ay me! but yet thou mightst my seat forbear . . .
>
> [*Sonnets*, XLI]

Yet Shakespeare fears the loss of his young friend's affection more than the loss of the woman he loves.

Both are now touched with ill report, Shakespeare by the 'vulgar scandal' stamped upon his brow by Greene's attack on him as a common player presuming to purloin the feathers of acknowledged writers. This he could support, 'so you *o'er-green* my bad, my good allow'. But further scandal attaches to them both through their association with the questionable woman with her ill reputation. At the beginning Shakespeare forgives the young man his fault –

> No more be grieved at that which thou hast done . . .
> All men make faults –   [*Sonnets*, xxxv]

Shakespeare excuses him, taking the blame upon himself.

Then Shakespeare's deeper involvement with her besmirches him, and he is afraid that it will bring dishonour upon his patron:

> I may not evermore acknowledge thee,
> Lest my bewailèd guilt should do thee shame,
> Nor thou with public kindness honour me,
> Unless thou take that honour from thy name.
>
> [*Sonnets*, x xxvi]

So, apart from those public dedications, the relations within this circle remained private – too awkward and involved to make any more public than they were.

Who was this woman whose personality was so strong – well known to people, who did not approve of her, either – that it could have such disturbing effects?

We derive some information about her from the brilliant skit which the poet wrote this year, 1593, upon the circle, making fun of the Southampton theme, *Love's Labour's Lost*. In the play the young courtiers around the King of Navarre abjure the society of women for a year to give themselves up to study. The joke is all the better because Henry of Navarre – well known to Essex, and probably Southampton too – was a notorious womanizer. The names of the courtiers – Berowne (Biron), Longaville, Dumain – come from pamphlets printed in Field's shop in Blackfriars, followers of Navarre.

What completely corroborates the nature of this play – dating, circumstance, characters and all – is the perfectly obvious identification of the Spaniard, Don Adriano de Armado. In this very year there was at Essex House, of which Southampton was an intimate, an emissary from the Court of Navarre, Philip ii's ex-Secretary, the exiled Don Antonio Perez. This egregious person soon wore out his welcome, with his airs and graces, his rhetorical flourishes and self-importance. Once he had been really important; now he was rather a laughing stock to the young men of this circle. Here he is to the life:

> Our Court, you know, is haunted
> With a refinèd traveller of Spain;
> A man in all the world's new fashion planted,
> That hath a mint of phrases in his brain;
> One who the music of his own vain tongue
> Doth ravish like enchanting harmony;
> A man of compliments . . .
> In high-born words the worth of many a knight
> From tawny Spain.   [*Love's Labour's Lost*, i.i.174]

Anne Hathaway's home at Shottery

Berowne thinks that forgoing the society of women is nonsense: he is all in favour of women and nature. This was Shakespeare's view, and he includes a skit upon himself in his character of Berowne, a self-portrait:

> but a merrier man,
> Within the limit of becoming mirth,
> I never spent an hour's talk withal.
> His eye begets occasion for his wit;
> For every object that the one doth catch
> The other turns to a mirth-moving jest. ...
> [*Love's Labour's Lost*, 11.ii.166]

And so on, laughing at himself. Everybody agreed that Shakespeare was an amusing and witty man – obvious enough from his plays; Greene suggested a euphoric, self-confident personality, John Aubrey described him as 'a handsome well-shaped man, with a very ready and pleasant smooth wit'.

Berowne is in love with a lady markedly and unfashionably dark. His dark Rosaline is described by his King as 'black as ebony', to which her lover replies,

> Is ebony like her? O wood divine ...
> No face is fair that is not full so black.
> [*Love's Labour's Lost*, 1v.iii.247]

Indeed, if her brows are black, she was born to make black fair. It is the very language of the sonnets, where we learn a great deal more about her, her character and conditions, Shakespeare's utter and humiliating infatuation and the deplorable story of the affair, which began in 1592 and went on into 1593 to its sudden, despairing end.

Shakespeare describes this woman pretty completely for us in the sonnets. She is very dark, with black hair, eyes and brows; some did not think her beautiful, and she had a bad reputation. She was musical – her playing on the virginals added another gift to her powers of seduction. Proud and tyrannical, she treated him cavalierly, looking down on him and demeaning him in talk with others. Extremely temperamental, she was inconstant, false to him as to others, for she was promiscuous. Both were married and therefore adulterers; Shakespeare, candid as always, makes no excuse for himself: he is infatuated and cannot help himself.

He can hardly understand why she has such a hold upon him, against the evidence of his own eyes, apart from what others say of her. She has put a spell upon him, and with her inconstancy – now consenting, now refusing – drives him 'frantic–mad'. In the end she breaks the vow she had made in bed with him to continue the affair. She seems to have broken it off – we do not hear her point of view; touched by 'love's distemper' he goes off to Bath for 'remedy'. Bath was the regular resort for persons affected by venereal disease, which was rampant in that age. Shakespeare was afraid that his young patron might be affected. The son of Lord Chamberlain Hunsdon (shortly also to become patron of Shakespeare's Company) became the second Lord Hunsdon, who succeeded his father as Lord Chamberlain and sought remedy for his disease at Bath, but died of it.

Vice-Chamberlain
Sir Thomas Heneage

Henry Carey
Lord Hunsdon

ÆTATIS SVÆ 66
ANᵒ 1591.

Lord Chamberlain Hunsdon

35

Hæc est Regia illa totius Angliæ ciuitas LONDINVM ad flu-
uium Thamesin sita. Cæsari, vt plures exis timāt, Trinobantum
nuncupata, multarum gentium cōmertio nobilitata, exculta domib. ornata tē-
plis, excelsa arcibus, claris ingenijs, viris omnium artium doc trinarumq́, gene-
re præstantibus, percelebris. Deniq́, omnium rerum copia, atque opum excellēcia
mirabilis. Snuehit in eam totius orbis opes ipse Thamesis, onerarijs nauibus per
se xaginta millia passuum, ad vrbem præalto alueo nauigabilis.

Emilia Lanier of 27
yeares 1597 the [illegible]
[illegible] at 25 p.m. [illegible]

And wher her husband shall have
the suit. [illegible] for his husb. 2 40

Henry Ma[illegible] of
53 yeares 1597 the
[illegible] at 4 5 7 8 [illegible]

Emilia [illegible]

She seamed to be with
child 12 daies or 12
weekes more paine in the
left side [illegible]
[illegible]
[illegible] but the
conception will not stai
with her [illegible]

She hath many false conceptions

And she shall have the suit but
she shalbe first in dispaire of it

She was brought up with the Countes of
Kente & hath bin maried 4 yers
The old Lord Chamberlain kept her longe
She was maintained in great pomp. she
is high minded. she hath [illegible]
[illegible] she would have don for [illegible]
she hath 40£ a yere & was welthy
to him that maried her in mony & Jewells
She can hardly kepe secrets. she was very brave in youth. she hath many
false conceptions. she hath a son his name is Henry

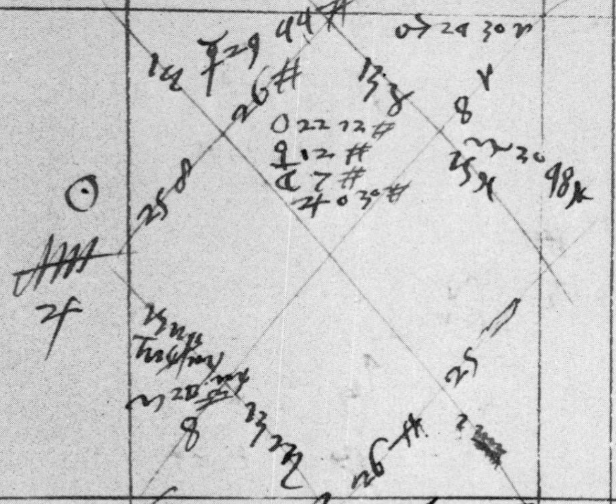

The circle was a very small one, in and around, or rather at the head of, the Lord Chamberlain's Company, which was being formed at this very time and was established on a permanent footing the very next year, 1594. Lord Hunsdon, a first cousin of the Queen, was the Lord Chamberlain of her Household; the Vice-Chamberlain was Sir Thomas Heneage, whom Southampton's mother was to marry on 2 May of that year. Richard Burbage, a key figure in the formation of the Company, was, with Shakespeare, to become a lifelong Fellow in it, and its star. He was the son of Cuthbert Burbage, for long the Lord Chamberlain's player.

The latter's son, the second Lord Chamberlain Hunsdon, lived in Blackfriars. Shakespeare was familiar with the Court from frequent performances there, though he had a line of information on its denizens and goings on through Southampton. In Blackfriars was his Stratford printer, Field, with his interesting list of foreign books. John Florio was Southampton's Italian tutor and household servant; Shakespeare's relation to it was not only that of poet and player, but on the independent footing of a gentleman, upon which he insisted.

One of the Queen's Italian musicians, Baptista Bassano, left a daughter Emilia by the Englishwoman with whom he lived as his 'reputed wife'. The girl had been born in 1569, and about the time of the Armada or just before – when the elderly Hunsdon came south from the Borders to head the Queen's bodyguard – he took the Italian girl, with her musical background, for mistress. He kept her in state; she told Simon Forman that she had received favour from the Queen, almost certainly earlier as the young orphan of her musician than as her cousin's mistress later. Many musical compositions were dedicated to the Lord Chamberlain; so perhaps her musical gift was an added attraction, or solace, to him too. She said that she had received favours from other lords also. No doubt.

In 1592 she became pregnant, and in October was married off 'for colour', in the usual fashion, to another of the Queen's musicians, Alphonso Lanier. Later we find that he was well known to Southampton, served on the Azores Expedition with him in 1597, and under Essex and Southampton in Ireland. When her child was born, it was named after the Lord Chamberlain, Henry. But Emilia was unhappy with her husband; she said that he spent her substance – the £40 a year with which she had been paid off and the jewels she had received for her services. She was miserable at having been cast down from the pomp in which she had been kept. Shakespeare tells us that his love for her – so like his nature – had begun out of pity for her condition; he appealed to her, humiliatingly:

> If thy unworthiness raised love in me,
> More worthy I to be beloved of thee.
> [*Sonnets*, CL]

Misfortune did not reduce her spirit; she became a bad lot – seductive as she was, she was a bitch. Three or four years later, in 1597, she behaved to Simon Forman, a great connoisseur of women and their ways, precisely as she had to William Shakespeare.[2] When her husband was away at sea, she bade Forman to her house at night, led him on, allowed him every liberty except

The Dark Lady consults Forman

[2] cf. my *Simon Forman: Sex and Society in Shakespeare's Age*, pp. 110 foll.

Southampton in the Tower

the last – behaviour which maddened him. She was now hard up, though she lived like a lady, with a manservant as well as a maid. Another time she commanded him to her house, and was willing to go further. Forman found her 'high minded', ambitious as ever, wanting to be a lady of title – her husband had gone to serve at sea in hopes of being knighted. Forman said roundly that he was not worthy thereof, neither was she; and he condemned her as 'a whore'. In the end she alarmed him – as no other woman in his very wide experience did: he wondered what to think of her tales concerning the conjuring of spirits.

This was an illicit and dangerous activity, though familiar enough to Elizabethans – as we have seen with Marlowe. In all this we do not have the woman's point of view; no doubt she considered that she had had a raw deal from life, and this sharpened the edge of her temper and ambition, her character formed by the shady and uncertain circumstances of her youth – left an orphan to fend for herself, elevated quite young to a dazzling but equivocal position, to be discarded and married off to a man she disliked.

To look at the matter from the woman's point of view, she had reason to distrust and despise men, and to treat them with something of what she had received at their hands. The temperament is recognizably Italian, and one can hardly blame her. It is evident that William Shakespeare, with his charming nature, was seduced by compassion as well as by the insatiable demands of sex. This sophisticated creature was a very different matter from a *Hausfrau* at Stratford, with no accomplishments.

What makes Forman's information so valuable is that we now have the ages of these people: this makes them real to us and throws a flood of light upon their relations. In 1592, when Emilia was discarded, and the affair with Shakespeare began, she was twenty-three, Southampton nineteen. Shakespeare was twenty-eight, no longer young for an Elizabethan – indeed his life was more than half over. One sees that Southampton, from Shakespeare's point of view, was liable to become her victim. No wonder he was driven to remorseful anxiety.

One also sees that, from her point of view, it was a bore being pestered by the infatuation of an impecunious actor, married and with a family to support. The lighter side to these relations *à trois* – the young Earl, his poet, Emilia – is to be seen in *Love's Labour's Lost*, with the King, Berowne, and the dark Rosaline. It has always been realized that this play was a private skit on a circle: this is the circle. The darker side of these relations, the obsession of lust, the guilt, treachery and remorse, are reflected immediately, in Shakespeare's way, in *The Rape of Lucrece*.

Later, we shall find it corroborated that Shakespeare's mistress was an altogether exceptional woman: not only musical, but of considerable literary cultivation with a wide range of Renaissance classic terms of reference. Two years after Thorpe published the *Sonnets*, with their blistering portrait of her, she replied with a volume of her own verse, showing herself the best woman poet of the age after Sidney's sister, the Countess of Pembroke.

4

The Lord Chamberlain's Company

OPPOSITE The principal actors in Shakespeare's plays
BELOW *A Midsummer Night's Dream,* first produced for the private wedding of Southampton's mother to Vice-Chamberlain Heneage, subsequently acted publicly by the Lord Chamberlain's Company

A
Midsommer nights dreame.

As it hath beene sundry times publickely acted, by the Right honourable, the Lord Chamberlaine his seruants.

Written by William Shakespeare.

¶ Imprinted at London, for *Thomas Fisher,* and are to be soulde at his shoppe, at the Signe of the White Hart, in *Fleetestreete.* 1600,

T THIS TIME the player–poet–dramatist – a 'perfect Johannes Factotum', as Greene had called him – was thinking of 'a summer story' and reading up in Chaucer. This was the origin of *A Midsummer Night's Dream,* but it grew to serve another purpose within the circle. The play celebrates the marriage of a stately, elderly couple. Since Southampton broke his promise to marry the Lord Treasurer's granddaughter – and was made to pay for it, financially and with loss of favour – his mother, the Countess, did what she could to protect the family's interests by marrying the elderly Vice-Chamberlain, Sir Thomas Heneage. The Queen may well have disapproved of her Vice-Chamberlain marrying the Catholic Countess, for it is known that Heneage was in disfavour in the early part of 1594, and not restored to favour until the end of the year. In these circumstances the wedding took place privately – one reason why scholars have had difficulty in identifying the ceremony for which the play was produced and adapted. But there need be no doubt about the event, for, though the play was conceived as a midsummer story, after the marriage of the elderly, stately couple, it turns out that the young people are returning from the jollifications of May Day. The Countess' wedding to the Vice-Chamberlain took place on 2 May 1594. This was the occasion of the play's performance.

A further touch relating it to the patron's circle is a passage describing a royal visit to a university, where speaking before the Queen dumbfounded some of the dons, made them 'shiver and look pale' and break off their speeches in confusion. On the Queen's visit to Oxford in the summer of 1592, Southampton was incorporated as Master of Arts; no doubt his poet was in attendance to watch the proceedings – *Love's Labour's Lost* has the university term for it:

> Proceeded well, to stop all good proceeding,
> [*Love's Labour's Lost,* 1.i.95]

from this non-university man.

The Workes of William Shakespeare,

containing all his Comedies, Histories, and Tragedies : Truely set forth, according to their first ORJGJNALL.

The Names of the Principall Actors
in all these Playes.

Illiam Shakespeare.

Richard Burbadge.

John Hemmings.

Augustine Phillips.

William Kempt.

Thomas Poope.

George Bryan.

Henry Condell.

William Slye.

Richard Cowly.

John Lowine.

Samuell Crosse.

Alexander Cooke.

Samuel Gilburne.

Robert Armin.

William Ostler.

Nathan Field.

John Underwood.

Nicholas Tooley.

William Ecclestone.

Joseph Taylor.

Robert Benfield.

Robert Goughe.

Richard Robinson.

Iohn Shancke.

Iohn Rice.

RIGHT Edward Alleyn,
who acted the leading roles in
Marlowe's plays

BELOW William Sly, a leading
actor in Shakespeare's Company

With the cessation of the plague in 1594 the theatre companies could come together again and, out of the confusion and uncertainty that had prevailed, establish themselves on a much firmer footing. Early in 1594 a strong combination was formed, upon the initiative of the Burbages, Hunsdon's men, to constitute the Lord Chamberlain's Company. Richard Burbage was to become their star, William Kemp their most celebrated comedian, William Shakespeare both player and playwright. With these were joined John Heming and Augustine Phillips; there followed Henry Condell, Thomas Pope and William Sly to form an inner group of Fellows, partsharers with the Burbages. This arrangement provided the lasting incentive which enabled the Chamberlain's Men to become the leading Company, beating the Admiral's Men with the initial advantage of their leading actor, Edward Alleyn, and Marlowe's plays to perform.

Nathan Field, a popular actor in the Lord Chamberlain's Company, who also wrote plays

Shakespeare brought to the new combination his own long, hard-won experience as actor, dramatist and producer, together with his shrewd business capacity which offers a contrast with his father's confused affairs. In June the Chamberlain's men and the Admiral's were playing together, or alternately, for a brief ten days; they did not co-operate again, but moved forward in bracing and fruitful competition. In the autumn the Chamberlain's Company went on tour; in October Hunsdon wrote to the Lord Mayor on behalf of his new company, that they might continue their occupation of the Cross Keys inn in the City. At Christmas they presented two plays at court – in all probability *Love's Labour's Lost* and *A Midsummer Night's Dream*, their dramatist's latest productions, which had not yet been seen there. In March next year Shakespeare received payment for them, with Richard Burbage and Kemp; henceforward the Company had the lead at Court.

It was his share in the Company, rather than payments for acting and writing plays, that provided the foundation of Shakespeare's ultimate independent fortune. Where did he get the money to purchase his share in it? From Southampton, according to the poet laureate in the next generation, Will Davenant, who liked it to be thought that he was a by-blow of Shakespeare's (they had several characteristics in common, besides poetry and the theatre).

Such a handsome present 'to go through with a purchase he had a mind to' was a proper reward for service and dancing attendance upon the young peer when called upon – at Southampton House in Holborn, near the Elizabethan houses that have miraculously survived there; at Titchfield Abbey ('bare ruined choirs'), his country house near Southampton; or, as we have seen, at Oxford, conveniently on the route to or from Stratford.

That Shakespeare chafed sometimes at the demands made upon him for attendance, the casual calls of the young peer upon his time, he tells us:

> Being your slave, what should I do but tend
> Upon the hours and times of your desire. . . .
> [*Sonnets*, LVII]

This is the way poets write, with a shade of irony in the exaggeration; all the same, there is the shadow of reproach:

Shakespeare's star actor
and Fellow: Richard Burbage,
self-portrait

> Nor dare I chide the world-without-end hour
> Whilst I, my sovereign, watch the clock for you.
>
> [*Sonnets*, LVII]

It is not for him to call the youthful patron to account for the way he spends his time:

> Being your vassal, bound to stay your leisure.
>
> [*Sonnets*, LVIII]

Now, with all the work involved in setting the Lord Chamberlain's Company on its feet, making the most of the security at last found, with all the opportunities to make the most of – acting, touring, performing at Court – the young Earl has reason to complain, Shakespeare admits:

> That I have frequent been with unknown minds,
> And given to time your own dear-purchased right. . . .
>
> [*Sonnets*, CXVII]

He is conscious that:

> Alas, 'tis true I have gone here and there,
> And made myself a motley to the view –

i.e. exposed himself as just an actor:

> Gored mine own thoughts, sold cheap what is most dear.
> [*Sonnets*, cx]

Needs must – and he expresses his resentment that he was not born to independent means, better prospects, surrounded by the friends, the scope and prospects the Earl possessed: the girding against his luck in life:

> That did not better for my life provide
> Than public means which public manners breeds.
> [*Sonnets*, cxi]

We see with what determination, against all setbacks, Shakespeare pursued the aim of independence, by his life of labour and concentrated work, after the prolonged apprenticeship, the handicaps of his birth and early marriage. And no less his fixation upon his quality as a gentleman: 'my name receives a brand' as a common player, and – what is worse, 'almost thence my nature is subdued to what it works in'.

With all these pressures upon him, Shakespeare never forgets what he owes to Southampton, recognizes:

> Wherein I should your great deserts repay,

and concludes the account of these momentous three years for him:

> Whereto all bonds do tie me day by day.
> [*Sonnets*, cxvii]

At the end of it all Shakespeare sums himself up with characteristic honesty and openness; he makes no excuses for his own nature, his weakness for women – a great strength to him as a dramatist (contrast Marlowe!). Other people are no better than he is:

> For why should others' false adulterate eyes
> Give salutation to my sportive blood?

He was free with women, more than normally addicted to them: why should that be accounted against him,

> Or on my frailties why are frailer spies,
> Which in their wills count bad what I think good?

He closes with the absolute affirmation that he is what he is, faults and all, and people must take him as such:

> No: I am that I am, and they that level
> At my abuses reckon up their own.
> [*Sonnets*, cxxi]

He rounds up the relationship with the Earl in similar terms of absolute candour. His feeling for him had not been on account of his being 'a child of state' – that is, a young peer, ward of the Lord Treasurer and all. It was nothing to Shakespeare that he had borne 'the canopy' – that was something 'extern', i.e. external, the proper 'outward honouring', appropriate decorum towards one of an Earl's rank. Inwardly, it had been a case of true affection; in taking leave, Shakespeare wished only to be 'obsequious in thy heart', to regard him with love, his only oblation, 'poor but free'. And then, last words of all, the magnificent affirmation of equality, man for man:

> But mutual render, only me for thee.   [*Sonnets*, CXXV]

WE HAVE REACHED the winter of 1594–5, as we know from the politico-religious references, in the penultimate Southampton sonnet CXXV, to the persecution of Jesuits and seminary priests which rose to a new height that winter. Shakespeare, as usual, shared the ordinary Englishman's patriotic viewpoint that they constituted a fifth column in time of war; they, of course, claimed that they were martyrs purely for their religion:

> the fools of time
> Which die for goodness which have lived for crime.
> [*Sonnets*, CXXIV]

(Both views were true enough: there were both sorts.)

Earlier that year there had been a great sensation over the Lopez affair, which we in our time have the worst of reasons for being able to understand (as the Victorians did not) – with its overtones of espionage and counter-espionage, international intelligence men and the ugly spectre of popular anti-Semitism. Dr Lopez, a Portuguese Jew, was the Queen's doctor, intelligent and highly successful, which made him envied; he was also conceited and ambitious, and took a hand in counter-intelligence work with and against Spain – and this was dangerous. What settled his hash was that he let it be known that Essex had a venereal disease – and Essex determined to frame him. We must remember that Southampton was Essex's devoted follower, who followed him to the edge of the scaffold.

Lopez was charged with undertaking to poison the Queen, for an enormous bribe from Spain. No doubt such a project was mentioned as bait, and Lopez was in touch with Spain. The Queen never believed him guilty of any such serious intention; but – like Soviet Russia today – if you could not prove your innocence in so dangerous a matter as treason, then you were held guilty in the England of Elizabeth I, 400 years ago. And Lopez could not prove his innocence of such communications. Essex was not only his accuser, but the judge at his trial, when he was – of course – condemned.

The Queen held out against the sentence being executed. The affair led to a popular outburst of anti-Semitism; Essex had popular feeling with him, as always. Lopez was condemned to death in February; the Queen resisted the execution for months, until her hand was forced by popular clamour, and the doctor was hanged in June. Shakespeare does not commit himself on this highly dubious issue, but his line

> The mortal moon hath her eclipse endured

THE EXCELLENT

Hiſtory of the Mer-

chant of Venice.

With the extreme cruelty of *Shylocke* the Iew towards the ſaide Merchant, in cut-ting a iuſt pound of his fleſh. And the obtaining of *Portia*, by the choyſe of three Caskets.

Written by W. SHAKESPEARE.

Printed by *J*. Roberts, 1600.

Shakespeare's *Merchant of Venice* was influenced by *The Jew of Malta* by his earlier rival, Marlowe

describes it, as might be expected, from the point of view of people in general: it means that, with the settlement of the issue, the Queen has emerged from the shadow upon her. It is really quite simple; while at the very same moment, the uncertainties abroad were settled:

> And peace proclaims olives of endless age.
> [*Sonnets*, CVII]

Henry of Navarre had won his final victory with the surrender of Paris in May 1594. The combination of the two events at one and the same time gives us certainty.

Southampton's friend,
Sir Henry Danvers

The players were quick to take their opportunities with the public, naturally – as we saw with Shakespeare's response to the Normandy campaign in 1591. The Lopez affair led to the revival of Marlowe's old play, *The Jew of Malta*: it was played more than fifteen times between the trial and the end of the year. The play belonged to the Admiral's Men; it was only natural that the Chamberlain's men should respond, and still more characteristic of their dramatist that he should take a leaf out of Marlowe's book and later go one better (what had Greene foretold?) with *The Merchant of Venice*. Shylock was the character everybody remembered: the play was sometimes referred to as 'The Jew of Venice'.

In October of 1594, when Southampton reached his majority, he was involved in an affair which must have increased his disfavour with the Queen. And indeed it was a shocking, sensational affair. For some time there had raged a bitter feud between two leading families down in Wiltshire, neighbours of Southampton: the Danverses of Dauntsey and the Longs of Wraxall. This culminated a couple of days before the Earl's birthday, on 4 October 1594, with the killing of Henry Long, son and heir of the family, by two young swordsmen, Sir Charles and Sir Henry Danvers, friends of Southampton – the latter rather more than a friend.

Southampton enabled them to make their getaway across the Channel to Henry of Navarre: he hid them in a lodge of his park at Titchfield, fed them, spent a night with them, and arranged their escape by boat. When the Sheriff came over Itchen Ferry, at the head of the hue and cry after them, a couple of the Earl's servants – one of them, 'Signor Florio, an Italian' – threatened to throw the representative of law and order overboard.

Again we do not have to look far for what shortly sparked off a play in the dramatist's imagination, ready to seize on any suggestion, any likely story – we see this throughout his work from beginning to end, from *Henry VI* right on to *The Tempest* and *Henry VIII*. Now, for next year, 1595, Shakespeare looks up a story with its Italian colouring, which combines friendship and love with feud and death, and produces *Romeo and Juliet*.

So concludes, for the time, the record of the most creative relationship of patron and poet that our literature provides. Of course, it was more, as Shakespeare tells us: a most significant meeting of minds and natures. The mimetic nature of actor and dramatist made the most of what fortune brought to him; more than that, his own nature, warm and honest, open and free, responded with gratitude and love to the inspiration which the golden youth with the generous nature offered. Everyone notices the importance of friendship in his creative work in consequence – the emotional friendship of Romeo and Mercutio (who may well have a suggestion of Marlowe in him), of Antonio and Bassanio in *The Merchant of Venice*. More important, the inner life and nature of our greatest writer was laid open in the sonnets – too intimately for publication; for they are his autobiography.

Nor need we look far for the Italian colouring of the plays, the Italian words and phrases. Within that close intimate circle was John Florio, the Earl's Italian tutor, during these years preparing his significant Italian–English dictionary, dedicated also to Southampton, but in the obsequious terms of a household servant, not the language of love, courteous but independent, of the dedication of *The Rape of Lucrece*. Behind that was the tempestuous experience with the Dark Lady, not only a recognizably Italianate temperament, but Italian by blood: Emilia Bassano.

5

Success

FTER THIS PERIOD of miraculous inner illumination, we must content ourselves with the external events of Shakespeare's life. There is nothing exceptional in that: it is all we have to go on with most Elizabethans, especially with the playwrights, of whom for the most part we know very little. We are uniquely fortunate to have the sonnets, since he was a dramatist; the only things comparable are the sonnets of Sidney and Spenser, or the love-poems of Donne (which are more difficult to clarify). We do not know less, but *more*, about Shakespeare than any other Elizabethan dramatist.

Henceforth the plays are all in all, as the theatre was his life. We have the record of his outer career and circumstances, his progress in his profession and in prosperity, above all in his work as a dramatist. Even the greatest poetry is to be found there, for the challenge of the stage, the conflicts of action and passion called out the deepest in this man who was first and last an actor.

We must always keep in mind something that was natural among people writing for the stage in those days – the capacity to turn out work with both hands, and of different kinds: comedies, histories, tragedies. There was no dispiriting over-specialization; the star among actors, Burbage, was also a painter, who could paint a speaking self-portrait or design a shield, for which his Fellow, the playwright, wrote the words.

At some time in the confusion of the plague years, when theatre people were hard put to it, their little groups broken up, forming and re-forming, Shakespeare was called in to revise a couple of scenes in a play on Sir Thomas More. It had been sketched out by Anthony Munday, with contributions by others, in the usual manner of several hacks collaborating to turn out something quick. In 1593 there was popular agitation against the immigrants coming into the country, and this recalled the 'Evil Mayday' riots of 1517, which More had dealt with as Sheriff of London. It was too ticklish a theme to be allowed on the stage; from Shakespeare's handling of it we see that he

The South bank, showing Shakespeare's Globe

53

could be trusted not to make trouble for the authorities – unlike Marlowe or Ben Jonson. All his sympathies were with order and good government: he well understood how thin is the crust of civilization and how easy it is for a society to break down, with all the more suffering in consequence. We recognize his handiwork from the marked superiority of his scenes; it appears that in them we have his handwriting, since, though the play was not performed, the manuscript was submitted to the censor, the Master of the Revels, and so has survived.

The playwright had a rich mine of material to hand in English history, which he could turn to at will in the new edition of Holinshed, his fellow Warwickshireman's *Chronicles*, brought out in 1587. Shakespeare also read Sir Thomas More's account of Richard III: More had been in an exceptionally favourable situation to know the inward truth of his *coup d'état*, having personally known some of the *dramatis personae*. This play provided the Chamberlain's Men with a tremendous star part for Burbage, and made such a hit that it registered in popular folklore in town and country – at Bosworth, for example. In London the tale went that a woman at the theatre made an assignation with Burbage, which his fellow actor overheard, got his stroke in first and was 'at his game ere Burbage came. Message being brought that Richard III was at the door, Shakespeare caused return to be made that William the Conqueror was before Richard III'.

Ben trovato; but it is likely enough, the kind of thing that happened at the theatre, and why not only Puritans but *bons bourgeois* disapproved. What it really shows us is that the names of the two leaders in the new company were becoming as well known as Tarleton had been before the plague years.

The writing of the play shows that Marlowe was still very much in his junior's mind: *Richard III* is the most Marlovian of his plays.

The fellowship within the Company was very close, as we see from their wills, regularly remembering their Fellows, bequeathing each other clothes and musical instruments – expensive items – and often a sum of money for a dinner to commemorate their good times together. Shakespeare's will is less intimate – simply money for Burbage, Heming and Condell to buy mourning rings. It is one more indication that he lived somewhat apart, in lodgings in London, his sights fixed on Stratford, where he meant to rehabilitate the family as an independent gentleman. Aubrey tells us that he was 'wont to go into Warwickshire once a year'; for the rest, very busy in London or on tour. He tells us that Shakespeare was 'not a company keeper ... and wouldn't be debauched' – obvious enough, or he would not have got through all that work; also that early on he lived in Shoreditch, where many theatre people lived, along with the foreign musicians, among them the Bassanos.

In these years, 1595 and 1596, the playwright was living in Bishopsgate, within the City Wall from Shoreditch. Here he was assessed for tax at £5, the usual rating for middle-class people with no substantial holding. It was a convenient location, for the Chamberlain's Men were playing at this time at the Theatre and the Curtain in Shoreditch, occasionally at the Cross Keys inn yard in Gracechurch Street, with perhaps a visit to the Swan, across the river on Bankside. Going down Bishopsgate into the City Shakespeare would pass Crosby Place, whence Richard III had executed his *coup d'état* – he needed no

Holinshed's *Chronicles*, the source of Shakespeare's English history plays

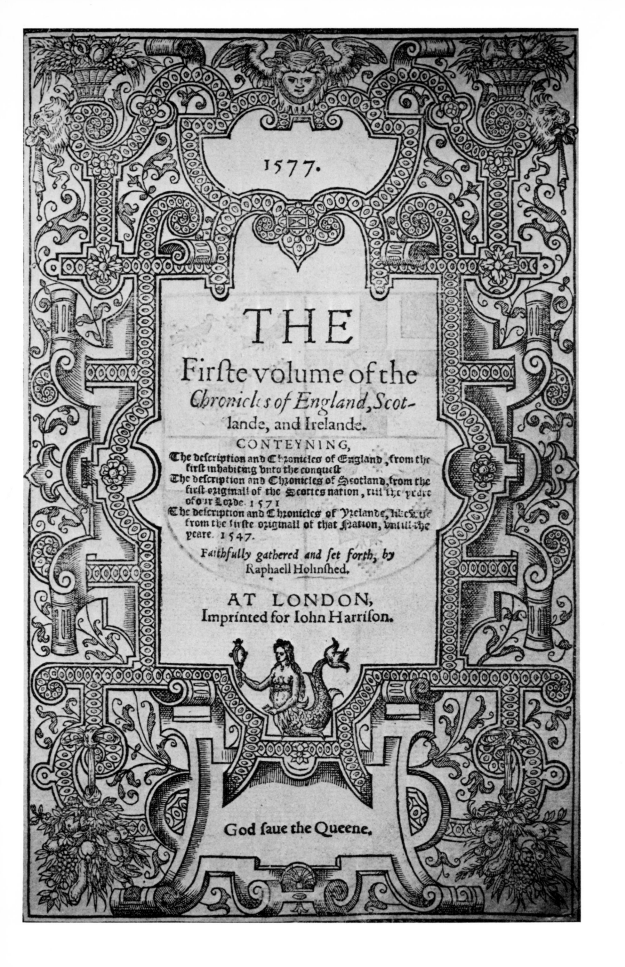

1577.

THE

Firste volume of the
Chronicles of England, Scot-
lande, and Irelande.

CONTEYNING,

The description and Chronicles of England, from the
first inhabiting vnto the conquest
The description and Chronicles of Scotland, from the
first originall of the Scottes nation, till the yeare
of our Lorde. 1571
The description and Chronicles of Yrelande, likewise
from the firste originall of that nation, vntill the
yeare. 1547.

Faithfully gathered and set forth, by
Raphaell Holinshed.

AT LONDON,
Imprinted for Iohn Harrison.

God saue the Queene.

The picture here set down
within this letter T:
A right doth shew the forme
of Tharlton vnto the shap

When hee in pleasant wise
the Counterfet exprest
of Clowne wt cote of russet
and sturtups wt ý reste, hew.

Whoe merry many mad
when he appeard in sight
The graue and wise as well as
at him did take delight, riue.

The partie nowe is gone,
and closlie clad in claye,
Of all the Iesters in the lande
he bare the praise awaie.

Now hath he plaid his pte
and sure he is of this.
If he in Christe did dieto liue
wth him in lasting blis.

Tarleton, most famous of
early Elizabethan comedians

reminder of the event. Below that came Gracechurch Street, with the Cross Keys. Another inhabitant of the parish at this time was the brilliant musician Thomas Morley, who set 'It was a lover and his lass'. By next year Shakespeare had moved across the river to Southwark, whence he belatedly paid his tax.

Besides playing at the public theatres, on tour, and in productions at Court, there were private performances and others for special occasions – what a harried, busy life it must have been when one thinks of all the memorizing, for the companies were repertory companies, with a number of plays ready to perform and others in rehearsal! Of the earlier plays, *The*

Taming of the Shrew had been performed out at Newington Butts, beyond Southwark, in June 1594, immediately upon the Chamberlain's Company being formed. During the Christmas festivities *The Comedy of Errors* had been played before the Queen at Court at Greenwich on Innocents' Day; and in the evening of that day – imagine the players in their barge coming up river with the tide – in the hall of Gray's Inn as part of their Christmas revels. On the second Grand Night, 28 December, there was such crowding on the dais that all was confusion: 'a Comedy of Errors (like to Plautus' *Menaechmi*) was played by the players – so that night was begun and continued to the end in nothing but confusion and errors. Whereupon, it was ever afterwards called "The Night of Errors".'

On 9 December 1595 Sir Edward Hoby, whose wife was the Lord Chamberlain's daughter, invited Sir Robert Cecil to his house in Canon Row, Westminster, 'where, as late as shall please you, a gate for your supper shall be open, and King Richard present himself to your view'. 'Readily', minuted the great little Secretary. Naturally a play of the Chamberlain's dramatist would be favoured by the family. In July next year, 1596, their patron, old Lord Hunsdon died; he was given a splendid funeral, and a very large monument in Westminster Abbey paid for by the Queen. He had held a lease of houses in Blackfriars; his son lived there, and hoped to succeed his father as Lord Chamberlain. The post was given to the elderly seventh Lord Cobham; he conveniently died, however, in March 1597, when the second Hunsdon achieved it, and with it the patronage of the Company.

The plays the Company's dramatist put forth in these two years, 1595 and 1596, are clear: *Romeo and Juliet* with one hand, *Richard II* with the other; followed by *King John* on the one hand, and then *The Merchant of Venice* on the other. Two plays a year were his usual output – nothing exceptional in that; many playwrights produced more, though his were of a higher quality – their popular appeal no less, in that age.

The starting point, and perhaps inspiration, of *Richard II* was again Marlowe: the Marlowe of his last and most mature play, *Edward II*, the story of a weak and ineffectual king, his deposition and final tragedy. But what a contrast with Marlowe's sinister thriller! Shakespeare's is all sympathy, lyricism and compassion. A quick-reading man – living on his own in London – he read up his sources, Holinshed, Hall's Chronicle and Froissart. To these he added Samuel Daniel's *The Civil Wars*, just out in 1595. The gifted and charming Daniel was rather close in spirit to him – his sonnets are for one thing; for another, both were historically minded, not only attracted by history but with real historical understanding, such as few literary men have. Daniel was almost as good an historian as he was a poet – few writers, surprisingly, have ever combined the two. He and Shakespeare certainly knew each other, for Daniel was brother-in-law to John Florio.

In pitting himself against Marlowe, and going beyond him now that he was dead, we are reminded of Ben Jonson's precise and pithy summing up of his evolution as a dramatist:

> how far thou didst our Lyly outshine,
> Or sporting Kyd, or Marlowe's mighty line ....[1]

---

[1] Ben Jonson's lines, 'To the Memory of my beloved, the Author, Mr William Shakespeare', prefaced to the First Folio.

How accurate that is! the player set himself to rival Lyly in the early comedies, *The Comedy of Errors* and *The Two Gentlemen of Verona*; the tragedian Kyd, in *Henry VI* and *Titus Andronicus*; and at length his only compeer in genius, Marlowe, with *Richard III* and *Richard II*. We see, too, how singularly poor Greene was being corroborated by this formidable competitor with the university wits. A mere player – and this play, too, like the sonnets and so many others of his works, has the self-reflective consciousness of the actor, as in a mirror:

> As in a theatre the eyes of men
> After a well-graced actor leaves the stage –

as it might be himself –

> Are idly bent on him that enters next,
> Thinking his prattle to be tedious.
> [*King Richard II*, v.ii.23–6]

King John followed close upon the heels of *Richard II*. Though not an inspired play like that one – Richard had something in him that appealed to Shakespeare's inner sympathy – there was a fine bravura part for Burbage in Faulconbridge, Richard Coeur-de-Lion's Bastard. Traditionally, Shakespeare was said to have taken 'kingly parts': here was one for him, and another for the Bastard's lean-faced legitimate brother. Several of these parts were written for the skinny Sinkler (or Sinclair): Justice Silence, Slender, Aguecheek. The comic parts were written for Kemp at this time; when he left the Company, he was succeeded by Robert Armin, a less boisterous type, more introvert, inclined to melancholy – hence the more refined parts written for the later Fools (Armin was a writer himself). There were parts for four boys – we appreciate now, as never before, how practically geared to the personnel of the Company and its resources was the work of this most practical, practising playwright. Once more, the theatre itself gets a salute: the men of Angers 'stand securely on their battlements, as in a theatre'. There they were, on the upper level.

A deeply touching passage – since his open nature expressed everything – was his grief at the death of his son Hamnet at Stratford, in August of 1596.

> Grief fills the room up of my absent child.
> Lies in his bed, walks up and down with me,
> Puts on his pretty looks, repeats his words,
> Remembers me of all his gracious parts,
> Stuffs out his vacant garment with his form. . . .
> [*King John*, III.iv.92]

A perceptive heart cannot but recognize the personal accents, the grief in the very rhythm of the verse.

That year also saw the grandest – and in its conduct, the most chivalric – exploit of the war: the capture of Cadiz. Lord Admiral Howard, Essex and Ralegh led it, and won glory; John Donne the poet served in it, as did Ralegh's brother-in-law, Arthur Throckmorton.[2] Southampton had to chafe at home; the Queen would not give permission for young peers, who

---

2 cf. my *Ralegh and the Throckmortons*, pp. 198 foll.

had no heirs to their peerages, to risk their lives. One of the rich Spanish galleons captured there makes its appearance in the play written at this time:

> And see my wealthy *Andrew* docked in sand,
> Vailing her high-top lower than her ribs –
> > [*The Merchant of Venice*, 1.i.27]

i.e. lowering her flag. More personal references that bespeak the author are his rueful observation, reflecting bitter experience:

> All things that are
> Are with more spirit chasèd than enjoyed.
> [*The Merchant of Venice*, 11.vi.13]

A play by Robert Armin, the comic actor of Shakespeare's later plays

That goes for the passionate pursuit of Emilia. There is his observation that bespeaks his passion for music, evident all through:

> The man that hath no music in himself
> Nor is not moved with concord of sweet sounds,
> Is fit for treasons, stratagems, and spoils.
> [*The Merchant of Venice*, v.i.83]

And religion? –

> In religion
> What damnèd error, but some sober brow
> Will bless it, and approve it with a text?
> [*The Merchant of Venice*, iii.ii.77]

There is the duplicity in things, the conflict between being and seeming, of which he was doubly conscious as an actor:

> There is no vice so simple but assumes
> Some mark of virtue on his outward parts.
> [*The Merchant of Venice*, iii.ii.81]

It is the doctrine of the sonnets.

After two years of hard work with his own Company Shakespeare at last felt firm ground under his feet and was beginning to taste the reward of success – independence. It was completely in character that he at once took up, in 1596, the negotiation for a coat-of-arms that had been dropped by his father twenty years before, when his affairs began to go wrong. The coat-of-arms was taken out in his father's name, so William could claim to be the son and heir of an armigerous gentleman. There was the familiar spear across a field of gold, the crest of a falcon spreading its wings, and the proud motto, never more justified: 'Non sanz droict'. The grant specified that it was for John's grandfather's 'faithful and valiant service' to Henry VII. Had he been at Bosworth, or was some imaginative person drawing the longbow? It recited that John had married one of the daughters of Robert Arden, 'esquire': this Arden may have been able to sign himself 'gentleman', but never 'esquire'. William Shakespeare did not rise into that category; he remained simply, but is always addressed respectfully, as 'gentleman'. To Elizabethans, with their carefully ordered society, these matters were significant; naturally a democratic society, a society in deliquescence, finds it difficult to understand them and to interpret the subtleties of Shakespeare's social scene.

Shakespeare was the first of his profession to acquire a coat-of-arms, an outward and visible sign of success and confidence in the future. Later he was followed by others of his Fellows in the Company, Phillips and Pope, while derisory Ben Jonson laughed at people putting down good money so that they could write themselves 'Gentlemen', with a coat of a Boar's Head looking like 'Hog's Cheek and Puddings in a Pewter field'. For motto he suggested, 'Not without mustard', for crest, 'A frying pan hath no fellow'. He must have chivvied Shakespeare with that, who no doubt took it in good part.

Shakespeare followed this up by buying about the finest house in Stratford, Hugh Clopton's five-gabled house with its little court in front,

Shakespeare's coat-of-arms

NON SANS DROICT

just across from the Guild Chapel he had often attended as a boy at school. (The house was rebuilt in the early eighteenth century, then that was pulled down too, leaving the vacant space with the cellars and two wells in what had been the inner courts, which we see today.) The house had been in need of repair, for the provident new householder sold the town a load of stone next year. Two barns, two orchards and gardens were attached; a few years later he bought a cottage and garden on the other side of Chapel Lane. The family settled in in 1597; next year he was holding ten quarters of malt there. Trading in malt was a regular business among leading townsmen; in 1604 he sold twenty bushels to a neighbour, lending him also a small sum of money. Since the neighbour did not pay up, William – more careful about money than his father, from whose experience he had himself suffered – put the offender through the town court and collected the debt.

With his affairs at last prospering, he was looking for a permanent investment in land – but not in London, as was the usual case with theatre people who made money there. He was loyal to Stratford, above all to his Arden inheritance. In 1597 his father and he offered the Lamberts the £40 for which Mary Arden's land at Wilmcote had been mortgaged; but the land was now worth more, and they could not get it back. Mary Arden's son had to look elsewhere for a solid investment of his savings. His neighbours, lawyer Sturley – agent of the Lucys out at Charlecote – and the Quineys, his father's associates on the borough council, tell us that William wished to purchase land at Shottery, his wife's old home. These friends were well disposed to advancing his interests, making his purchases of property in his own home town. They thought it would do the town a good turn if a local man bought the tithes, a considerable part of the endowment of the former college of priests, where, since the Reformation, his neighbours and friends, the Combes, had seated themselves.

In the autumn of 1598 Richard Quiney, stopping in London at the Bell in Carter Lane, near St Paul's, and finding himself short of cash, addressed a letter to William, his 'Loving Countryman', for a loan of £30. The letter was not delivered, but I detect a note of doubt whether he would succeed in raising money from his loving countryman. This is corroborated by lawyer Sturley's view of the proposition that 'our countryman, Master William Shakespeare ['Master' was a term of respect], would procure us money – which I will like of as I shall hear when, where, and how'.

Master Shakespeare had learned the hard way, and was taking his time. It was not until 1602 that he made his purchase: 107 acres of the best land in Old Stratford, for the considerable sum of £320. (Multiply by perhaps fifty; or, otherwise, what would over a hundred acres in Old Stratford be worth today?) The prosperous dramatist was too busy away to take seisin of his land; his brother Gilbert did it for him. Three years later, in 1605, William made a larger purchase, for £450, of one half of all the tithes – the tenth of the produce, which had gone to the upkeep of the canons of Stratford church (where we still see their stalls in the choir) – on wool, grain, grass and hay in Old Stratford, Bishopton and Welcombe; and the tithes on wool, lamb and smaller produce in Stratford parish. The tithes alone, apart from rents, brought in £60 a year (multiply again); they were farmed for the busy dramatist by Anthony Nash, whose son Thomas married Shakespeare's granddaughter and ultimate heiress, Elizabeth, subsequently Lady Barnard.

We see Shakespeare's tenacious social aspirations completely fulfilled, no less than his long-term literary ambitions – both overlooked by people not knowing what Elizabethans were like, how they operated, or the conditions in which they worked. With these purchases he was an independent gentleman, able to live at what became New Place; and his continuing returns from the theatre enabled him later to purchase a house in Blackfriars.

In this year in which he bought New Place, 1597, he was writing the two parts of *Henry IV*, the peak of his achievement in the *genre* of the chronicle play. They follow upon *Richard II*, and were followed by *Henry V*, the series linking up with the three on *Henry VI*. We see the forward-reaching character of his planning in his work, as in regard to his establishment at Stratford. Here we are concerned not with the literary aspect, but with the biographical one. We must, however, notice that, with Falstaff, he created the greatest comic character in our literature; and that, with his patent for history plays – the mixture of straight history with invented characters, like Falstaff, Fluellen, Faulconbridge – they were the ultimate origin of the proliferating historical novel.

The part of Falstaff would have been taken by the rollicking, boisterous Will Kemp – always a hit with the public. The character had originally been

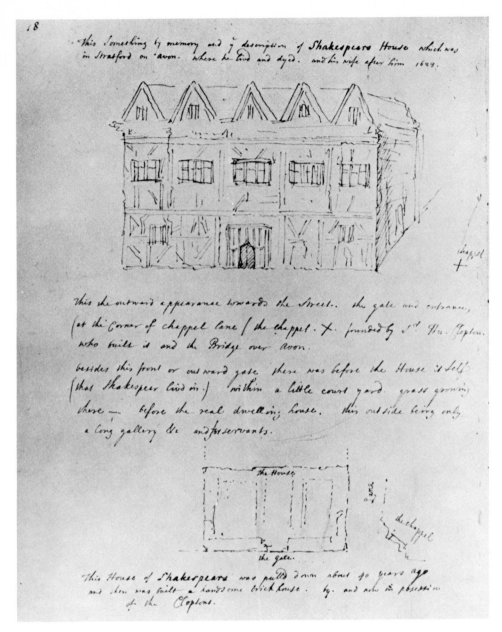

named Oldcastle, and this led to trouble with the Cobhams. The eighth Lord Cobham, who succeeded to the title that year, was a fool, and objected to the portrayal of Sir John Oldcastle as a buffoon on the stage – Oldcastle had married a remote Lady Cobham. Cobham was the brother-in-law of Robert Cecil and friend of Ralegh, to whom Essex and Southampton were bitterly opposed; so this caricature of a tunbelly carried further overtones to these enemies.

Next year, when Essex wrote that some maid-of-honour was marrying 'Sir John Falstaff', it was apparently meant against Cobham, who was a buffoon, or at least a nitwit. A year later, Southampton's wife – he had at last been caught – was writing him a joke to make him laugh (he was in Ireland and needed it), to the effect that Sir John Falstaff was made father 'by his mistress, Dame Pintpot, of a goodly miller's thumb, a boy that's all head and

The Guild Chapel at Stratford

very little body'. Did this, too, refer to Lord Cobham? Evidently the character of Falstaff was not only a favourite in the circle of Essex and Southampton, but carried some further implications. Though the period of patronage was over and Shakespeare was independent, he was their dramatist; this was his alignment.

These plays are full of a new sense of London life, for which he had evidently fallen: the talk of the carriers, quite Dickensian, the rowdy, riotous, bawdy characters, the authenticity of the scenes at the Boar's Head (recall Ben Jonson's joke), the hostess and the prostitute – it is all like Simon Forman's actual London: they totally corroborate each other. There are nostalgic scenes from the Cotswolds, too: Justice Shallow's house and orchard, with his reminiscences of Will Squeal, a Cotswold man, the red-nosed innkeeper of Daventry, old Puff of Barcheston (where the Sheldon tapestries were made). It links up with the Stratford background of Christopher Sly in *The Taming of the Shrew*.

This is reinforced in *As You Like It*, of 1598, with country characters from his own observation, while the Forest of Arden itself is suggested on the stage. The action of the play develops from the gentility theme. A younger brother is defrauded of his rights by an elder: 'My father charged you in his will to give me good education: you have trained me like a peasant, observing and hiding from me all gentleman-like qualities.' By an old tradition the part of the faithful family retainer, Adam, was taken by the dramatist.

What is most remarkable to us is that there are no fewer than three direct references to Marlowe. In this year the splendid poem *Hero and Leander* – which he had been writing in rivalry with *Venus and Adonis* for Southampton's favour when he was killed – was at last published, completed in very different style by Chapman, and with a touching preface by the publisher Edward Blount. (Blount was a friend of Thomas Thorpe, who ultimately got the manuscript of the sonnets and published them with *his* dedication to Mr W.H.) In the play Shakespeare makes his only direct reference to a contemporary, virtually naming Marlowe by quoting his well-known line:

> Dead shepherd, now I find thy saw of might:
> 'Who ever loved that loved not at first sight?
> [*As You Like It*, III.v.82]

There is a whole passage about Hero and Leander, and finally the recognizable reference to stupidity striking 'a man more dead than a great reckoning in a little room'. The coroner's inquest at Deptford stated that the quarrel in the little room in the tavern there was over 'le reckoning'. William Shakespeare would have known all about how Marlowe met his end.

Much Ado About Nothing, also of this time, has less biographical interest for us, though it has country touches, and the local humour of Dogberry and Verges, the parish constable and headborough. Aubrey tells us that Shakespeare and Ben Jonson 'did gather humours of men daily wherever they came', and that the humour of the constable was drawn from such a one at Long Crendon in Buckinghamshire – likely enough: it is on the direct route between London and Stratford. The parts of Dogberry and Verges were taken by Kemp and Cowley. Kemp left the Company shortly after to perform his famous dance, for a wager, all the way from London to Norwich.

In that year, 1598, there appears upon the scene a striking and formidable personality henceforth to be important in Shakespeare's story: Ben Jonson. Left fatherless, with an unsympathetic bricklayer for stepfather, he had come up a harder way than Shakespeare with his good family background; but Ben received a better education at Westminster School under Camden, though he also did not go on to university. Like Shakespeare he improved himself by self-education; much less good as an actor, he was even more of a reader: his cast of mind was intellectual, satirical, scholarly. Though he wrote for the theatre he was not a professional – unlike Shakespeare, a professional to his fingertips – or such men as Heywood, Fletcher, Massinger and Shirley. He wrote a certain amount for the boys' companies,

Ben Jonson

EVERY MAN IN
his Humor.

As it hath beene sundry times
publickly acted by the right
Honorable the Lord Cham-
berlaine his seruants.

Written by BEN. IOHNSON.

Quod non dant proceres, dabit Histrio.

Haud tamen inuidias vati, quem pulpita pascunt.

Imprinted at London for *Walter Burre,* and are to
be sould at his shoppe in Paules Church-yarde.
1601.

Ben Jonson's first play for
the Lord Chamberlain's Company,
in which Shakespeare acted

and ultimately moved into writing Court masques for magnificent productions by Inigo Jones.

Ben's character stood in marked contrast with that of his senior by eight years. Where Shakespeare was suave and courteous, affable and gentlemanly, Ben was rude and rumbustious, aggressive and pedantic; underneath this exterior, he was a good sort, with a warm heart, he was generous, and he, too, possessed genius. Belonging to a different generation and holding different views of the stage – didactic, moreover – he did not see eye to eye with his senior, and often criticized him. But it is obvious that Ben could not resist him; after his death the most generous and discerning tributes to Shakespeare's irresistible genius came from him.

67

Queen Elizabeth I in a Garter
Procession at Windsor

Now, in 1598, Shakespeare gave him his chance upon the public stage by
taking on his play, *Every Man in His Humour*, for the Company, and himself
performing in it. His name comes first in the list of the 'principal comedians',
the first extant list we have of the Chamberlain's Men. There they all are:
'Will. Shakespeare, Aug. Phillips, Hen. Condell, Will. Sly, Will. Kemp, Ric.
Burbage, Joh. Heming, Tho. Pope, Chr. Beeston, Joh. Duke.' These last
two lived in Shoreditch, but left the Company in 1602. Shakespeare did not
act in the sequel, *Every Man out of His Humour*, but he did in *Sejanus*, Jonson's
highly intellectual classic tragedy. This play had no success with the public,
nor had *Catiline*. This irritated Ben, when Shakespeare's classic vein with
Julius Caesar was so successful. However, Ben's greatest comedies, *Volpone*
and *The Alchemist*, were written for the Company; then he quarrelled with it,
as he usually did with everyone at some time or other.

Shakespeare's favour with the public was now reflected in the demand for versions of the plays in print – any version that could be put together from memory by an actor or two, rather than none at all. It was not to the interest of the Company to have the repertory it drew upon printed and broadcast, and it was not the practice of professionals to publish their plays, Shakespeare any more than any other. Ben Jonson was singular in this respect: his attitude was not that of a professional theatre-man; he thought himself – like Daniel or Drayton, though they occasionally wrote for it – above it. When he published his plays in folio, later, as his *Works*, he was laughed at. Shakespeare had no interest in printing plays, indeed his business interest was rather against it. But when too bad a version of a play was got hold of and published, the only remedy an author had was to publish a better – the copyright situation was different then.

Thus, when a poor version of *Romeo and Juliet*, put together from memory, appeared in 1597, next year a good one, 'newly corrected, augmented and amended' was put out, evidently from within the Company. A similar thing happened with *Love's Labour's Lost*; a fresh issue gave opportunity for revision and improvements. Sometimes a good text appeared close on the heels of its performance, as with the first part of *Henry IV* in this year. At the same time appeared a good text of the ever popular *Richard III*. The authentic texts of the Company's dramatist belonged to it, and remained with it; thus it is that, after his death, Heming and Condell published the plays in a large folio – following Ben Jonson's example – as an exceptional tribute to the memory of their fellow actor and dramatist.

In a summary account of English writers to date, a schoolmaster parson, Francis Meres, gave a useful list of Shakespeare's plays up to 1598. What is impressive is that he was the only writer to be mentioned in the section devoted to each *genre* – there again was the versatility noticed by Greene. As a writer for the stage, he is described as the English Plautus and Seneca, 'the most excellent in both kinds', comedy and tragedy. He is again placed among the best lyric poets, and the most passionate love-poets; he figures also among those who have greatly enriched and elaborated the language. True enough – and the language just then was in the most sensitive condition to respond, flexible, unsettled, expanding its horizons, like the country.

Other tributes were coming to be laid at his feet, and, what was gratifying, from both universities. The grandest accolade came from the highest quarter: the Queen expressed a desire to see Sir John Falstaff in love. Shakespeare's plays were familiar to her from the many performances of her Lord Chamberlain's Men at Court – they were now without question the premier Company. He, in turn, had been present on occasions when she spoke, in her shrill authoritative voice, and witnessed the impression she made:

> there is such confusion in my powers,
> As after some oration fairly spoke
> By a belovèd prince, there doth appear
> Among the buzzing, pleasèd multitude:
> Where every something, being blent together,
> Turns to a wild of nothing save of joy.
> [*The Merchant of Venice*, III.ii.180]

The Queen's wish was a command; it was evidently complied with in some haste, for *The Merry Wives of Windsor*, written for a Garter Feast at the Castle, is mostly in prose. Shakespeare was familiar with the environs of Windsor, from performances there. Once more he had to change a name at the objection of Lord Cobham. For the prank of shutting up Falstaff in the dirty-clothes basket and tumbling him out in the river, Ford was disguised as Master Brooke, Cobham's family name, as everybody knew. Was the joke deliberate? The dramatist had to change it to Broome.

OPPOSITE Elizabeth Vernon, Southampton's wife

THE FACTION-FIGHTING at Court between the friends of Essex and Southampton, and those of Cecil and Ralegh, became more ulcerated as the Queen's reign drew to an end. In 1597 it was temporarily patched up in the interests of a great expedition to the Azores, with the aim of catching the Spanish treasure fleet from the Indies. At last Southampton got leave to go, and served gallantly in command of the *Garland*. Emilia Lanier's husband went as a gentleman volunteer, in hopes of a knighthood – they had been scattered freely and rendered cheap at Cadiz the year before.

At home Southampton had for some time been playing about with one of the Queen's maids of honour, Elizabeth Vernon, and was at last caught in the usual manner, as Ralegh had been by Elizabeth Throckmorton. Still the young man did not wish to marry; instead, he got leave to travel to France, where he could enjoy the company of the Danvers brothers, now serving under Henri IV, and hoped to go on to Italy with the younger one, of whom he was particularly fond. Meanwhile Elizabeth Vernon's pregnancy advanced, and at the last moment Essex, who was her cousin, prevailed on him to return secretly and marry her. The Queen was furious, as usual, at this affront to her authority, and threatened to send them to the Tower. Essex interceded for him, and he was merely consigned to the Fleet for a brief time.

His mother's second husband, old Sir Thomas Heneage, had died after a year of married bliss with the Countess. She was seeking a new husband in a young man, Sir William Harvey, one of the Cadiz knights. It was rumoured that he might be made Comptroller of the Queen's Household; but a connection with Southampton was not likely to advance him in that quarter. She strongly disapproved of the Earl's conduct, and seems to have disliked him. Now he quarrelled with his mother over her projected marriage, which he thought unsuitable; for a time he managed to hold it up, but around the end of 1598 or beginning of 1599 it took place secretly. We have no means of knowing the precise date as we have with her marriage to Vice-Chamberlain Heneage, and its celebration by her son's poet with *A Midsummer Night's Dream*.

Elizabeth Countesse of Southampton; Vernon

❧ 6 ❧

The Fall of Essex and Southampton

HE LAST YEARS of the Queen's reign were rendered unhappy, and even critical, by resistance in Ireland reaching a new height in Ulster, the necessity of sending a full-scale army under Essex there, his humiliating failure and return to engage upon a course of conspiracy, involving Southampton with him, his open outbreak into the City, their trial and sentence to death. Essex's sentence was carried out, Southampton's suspended for imprisonment in the Tower for what remained of the Queen's life. Crowding, critical events; the ulcerated conflict of factions at Court and in London; the ruin of men's hopes of Essex; the misery and bitterness of it – all this is reflected, not obscurely, in the most sensitive register of the age. Shakespeare was close to these events, but naturally they are glossed in his work, in such a way that they could incur no trouble from the authorities. The deposition scene in *Richard II*, however, was not allowed to be printed so long as the Queen lived; not until James was securely established on the throne, and danger over, was it permitted to appear.

Irish resistance found its greatest leader in the Ulster chieftain, Hugh O'Neill – to the English, Earl of Tyrone. In 1598 he had inflicted the gravest defeat English forces had met with, at the disaster of the Yellow Ford. There was danger of Spain's intervention; it was necessary to send the largest army yet equipped for Ireland. Essex made it impossible for anyone else to assume the command, though the Queen had a better candidate; he was determined to make Southampton his General of Horse, though she vetoed it.

Shakespeare was writing *Henry V*. As usual throughout his career, from earliest *Henry VI* to latest *The Tempest* and *Henry VIII*, he responds to what is going on at the time, as a shrewd box-office head would – the atmosphere, the activity, the sense of expectancy, the events themselves. *Henry V* is an intensely patriotic play, as *Henry VI* had been with the Normandy campaign to the fore. Now it is Ireland, with Essex again. He is given a grand salute across the Irish Sea, with all the hopes that rested on him:

OPPOSITE Southampton's leader, Robert, Earl of Essex
BELOW *Richard II*: title page

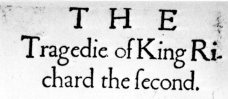

THE
Tragedie of King Ri-
chard the second.

As it hath beene publikely acted by the Right Honourable the Lord Chamberlaine his
seruants.

By William Shake-speare.

LONDON
Printed by Valentine Simmes for Andrew Wise, and
are to be sold at his shop in Paules churchyard at
the signe of the Angel.
1598.

73

> Were now the General of our gracious Empress –
> As in good time he may – from Ireland coming,
> Bringing rebellion broachèd on his sword,
> How many would the peaceful city quit
> To welcome him!   [*King Henry V*, Prologue. v.30]

Shakespeare's view was that of ordinary English folk, his patriotism that of the normal Elizabethan.

Essex had been given a grand send-off by the City in March 1599:

> How London doth pour out her citizens!
> The Mayor and all his brethren in best sort,
> Like to the senators of the antique Rome,
> With the plebeians swarming at their heels,
> Go forth and fetch their conquering Caesar in. . . .
> > [*King Henry V*, Prologue. v.24]

We see that a play on Julius Caesar is already forming in the double-minded dramatist, probably from his reading up for it.

Here was the activity in London, Essex's the best-equipped army to leave these shores during the reign:

> The armourers, accomplishing the knights –
> > [*King Henry V*, Prologue. IV.12]

'accomplishing', what a proud word, so like him! –

> With busy hammers closing rivets up,
> Give dreadful note of preparation. . . .
> > [*King Henry V*, Prologue. IV.13]

And the shipping necessary for so large an army:

> behold the threaden sails,
> Borne with the invisible and creeping wind,
> Draw the huge bottoms through the furrowed sea.
> > [*King Henry V*, Prologue. III.10]

Henry V was ready for performance when the Chamberlain's Men made their move from north London to the more convenient south bank, where they built their historic Globe Theatre. The Burbages demolished the Theatre in Shoreditch which had served the Company well, and transported the timbers across the Thames for their new house, the finest and largest to date, which expressed to the world (who thought of the new, challenging name, the Globe?) the primacy the Company had won for itself. It held perhaps 2000 packed in the pit open to the weather, the galleries all round sheltering those willing to pay more. A larger stage than the average today jutted right out among the audience, who were thus excitably caught up in the action they beheld three-dimensionally. Moreover, the action was continuous: no changes of scene meant that it was much more rapid, the impact far stronger, and mercurial, excitable Elizabethans were enraptured. Hence, too, Shakespeare's love affair with the audience, like Dickens' with his public – as against Ben Jonson's surly reaction.

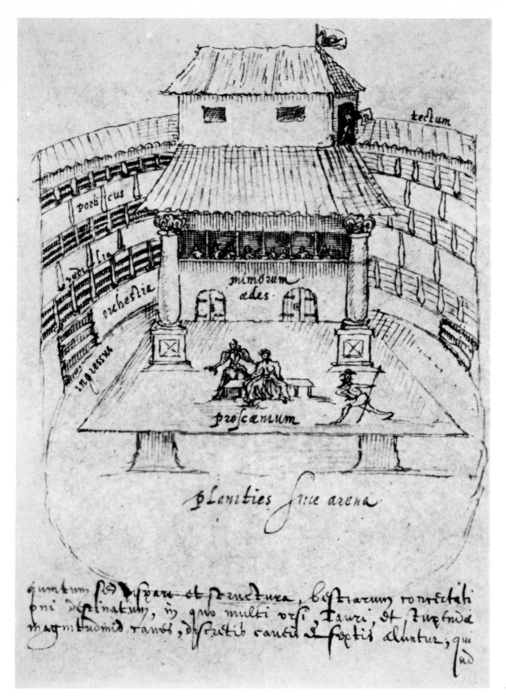

Henry V has Shakespeare's characteristic and constant wooing of the audience, his courteous (and cleverer) courting of their favour:

> But pardon, gentles all –   [*King Henry V*, Prologue. 1.8]

i.e. gentlemen and ladies, a polite way of addressing the Tom, Dick and Harry of an Elizabethan audience –

> The flat unraisèd spirits [indeed!] that hath dared
> On this unworthy scaffold to bring forth
> So great an object. . . .
> [*King Henry V*, Prologue. 1.9]

LEFT Interior of an
Elizabethan theatre
ABOVE The Globe Theatre

And then, with a look round the circular Globe itself –

> Can this cockpit hold
> The vasty fields of France? or may we cram
> Within this wooden O the very casques
> That did affright the air at Agincourt?
> [*King Henry V*, Prologue. 1.11]

Since this is a very different play from *Henry IV* and lacks its dramatic conflict of father and son, the diverse action of the war in France is drawn together by a Chorus, which plays a larger part than in any of his other plays. This speaks a very personal note, again requesting the sympathy of the audience for the impossibility of rendering the vast actions of war on the stage – and we ourselves see him playing it:

Plutarch's *Lives*, source of Shakespeare's Roman Plays

THE LIVES
OF THE NOBLE GRE-
CIANS AND ROMANES, COMPARED
together by that graue learned Philosopher and Historiographer, Plutarke of Chæronea:

Translated out of Greeke into French by IAMES AMYOT, Abbot of Bellozane, Bishop of Auxerre, one of the Kings priuy counsel, and great Amner of Fraunce, and out of French into Englishe, by

Thomas North.

Imprinted at London by Thomas Vautroullier and Iohn VVight.
1579.

Admit me Chorus to this history,
Who, prologue-like, your humble patience pray,
Gently to hear, kindly to judge, our play.
              [*King Henry V*, Prologue. 1.32]

Again, he speaks the Epilogue in his own person:

Thus far, with rough and all-unable pen,
Our bending author hath pursued the story. . . .
           [*King Henry V*, Epilogue. 403]

'Rough and all-unable pen' – again how like him! We must not assume that this is what he really thought; he had plenty of confidence in himself, and it was just his way of putting it.

The theatres were one of the chief attractions for foreign visitors, and a young Swiss, visiting London that autumn, tells us what performances at the Globe were like. He saw *Julius Caesar*:

... with a cast of some fifteen people. When the play was over, they danced marvellously and gracefully together: as is their wont, two dressed as men and two as women. Daily at two in the afternoon London has two, sometimes three plays running in different places ... Whoever cares to stand below pays one English penny, but if he wishes to sit he enters by another door and pays another penny; if he desires to sit in the most comfortable seats, which are cushioned, where he not only sees everything well but can also be seen, then he pays yet another English penny at another door. During the performance food and drink are carried round the audience. The actors are most expensively and elaborately costumed.

With the cycle of subjects that appealed to him in Holinshed virtually complete, Shakespeare turned to new territory opened up by North's translation of Plutarch's *Lives* – the field of Roman history. This book had been originally issued by Vautrollier from Blackfriars; Richard Field succeeded to it, when he took over the widow and her business, and printed the several editions that came out in Shakespeare's lifetime. A quick reader, Shakespeare turned also to Marlowe's translation of Lucan and Kyd's translation of Garnier's *Cornelia*; while he was also reading Daniel's *Musophilus*, a fine poem just out. Shakespeare characteristically picks up a thought and a phrase from Daniel's imaginative forecast of the future of the English language overseas.

And who in time knows whither we may vent
The treasure of our tongue, to what strange shores
This gain of our best glory shall be sent
To enrich unknowing nations with our stores?
What worlds in the yet unformèd Occident
May come refined with the accents that are ours?[1]

Shakespeare naturally translates this into dramatic terms:

How many ages hence
Shall this our lofty scene be acted over
In states unborn and accents yet unknown!
           [*Julius Caesar*, III.i.111]

[1] Samuel Daniel, 'Musophilus', ll.957 foll.

Had he any idea that he himself would be a prime agent in the process?

Julius Caesar again offered something quite different: its author's conception of the classical, no sub-plot, no comic relief whatever. Grave and austere, it is yet alive and exciting all through, and greatly appealed to the public. This irritated Ben Jonson more than any of his senior's efforts, his own classical plays, weighed down by scholarly pedantry, falling dead. Ben made jokes against *Julius Caesar* several times in his own works; one lapse which Shakespeare had committed, 'Caesar did never wrong but with just cause', was emended in the text by the time the Folio came out.

We need note nothing personal in the work, except Shakespeare's contemptuous rendering of the mob, regular with him – and the Elizabethan audience did not resent it. Equally regular are his references to the theatre: 'if the tag-rag people did not clap him and hiss him [Mark Antony] according as he pleased and displeased them, as they used to do players in the theatre. . . .' Note the joke, 'used to do'!

MEANWHILE, WITH ESSEX IN IRELAND, all was humiliation and fiasco, turning to worse – treason. From the first he was in no mood to do the job he was sent to do; he wasted precious time, and engaged in an angry correspondence with the Queen about Southampton. When they arrived in Ireland Essex used his full authority as Lord Lieutenant to appoint him Lord General of Horse. The Queen over-ruled him, and gave her crisp opinion of Southampton: 'We . . . did expressly forbid it, being such a one whose counsel can be of little, and experience of less, use.' She added a tart reminder of his recent misdemeanour with Essex's cousin: 'Were he not lately fastened to yourself by an accident – wherein for our usage of ours we deserve thanks – you would have used many of your old lively arguments against him for any such ability of commandment.'

Actually the young man showed courage and gallantry in the field, though it was not his only form of gallantry. He had promoted a tough fighting captain, Piers Edmonds, with whom Essex too was familiar; he ate and drank, and lay in his tent with Southampton, who 'would cull and hug him in his arms and play wantonly with him'. War has its consolations no less than peace; while at home his wife, very much in love with him, regretted that she was not again pregnant, to provide him with a son and heir. That was to come; in the event, after the period of terrible danger he was to bring down upon himself, and his imprisonment in the Tower – it seems to have brought this spoiled child of fortune to his senses – he settled down to a notably happy family life. At last!

He was, however, present at the treasonable interview with the grand rebel, Tyrone, with which Essex brought to an end in fiasco all the hopes placed upon him. The unpardonable thing was that he discussed with the Irish chieftain what should be done about the succession to the Crown; he was hoping to use James from Scotland to bring pressure upon the Queen. She could never put her case to the public; so her popularity with the people suffered in consequence – Essex, who should have been her chief support, robbed her of it. But she knew her duty, as Queen, to a traitor – though, as a woman, to carry it out was heartbreaking.

After this deplorable upshot, Essex hurried back to throw himself at her feet. He was placed under house arrest, while the Southamptons took his place at Essex House, with Essex's sister (the Stella of Sir Philip Sidney's Sonnets earlier), where they kept open house to all the Essex faction. When they were sent packing, Southampton, with the youthful Earl of Rutland for company – another of the faction – 'passed their time merrily in going to plays every day'. Among the new plays to be seen were *Henry V* and *Julius Caesar*. Early in the new year, 1600, these lords were in London all the week 'and passed away the time in feasting and plays'. The Lord Chamberlain, the second Lord Hunsdon, was entertaining the Dutch envoy with his Company's *Henry IV*.

While Essex staggered on his unsteady course, half-heartedly gathering the threads of conspiracy against the Court, sick in mind and body, a psychotic case driven to the edge of desperation, Shakespeare was writing *Hamlet*. It has several traces of this anxious time, and some of what Essex had been in the eyes of his following and still was in the eyes of the people, who as usual did not know the situation as it really was:

> The courtier's, soldier's, scholar's, eye, tongue, sword;
> The expectancy and rose of the fair state ...
> The observed of all observers.   [*Hamlet*, III.i.59]

Francis, Earl of Rutland

There had been touches of his glittering personality before, notably in Bolingbroke's currying favour with the mob, as Essex had always done. Now,

> on his choice depends
> The sanity and health of this whole state –
>   [*Hamlet*, I.iii.21]

and he chose wrong. But he had the people with him:

> He's loved of the distracted multitude,
> Who like not in their judgment but their eyes.
>   [*Hamlet*, IV.iii.4]

Shakespeare never has a good word for the people as such: they seem to have respected him all the more for it.

The dramatist himself was torn in two. His intellectual sympathies were with authority, order and good government; but his personal alignment was with Southampton and his leader, Essex. Their dislike of the old Lord Treasurer, Burghley, may well be expressed in the prosy, moralizing Polonius, with his platitudinous, worldly-wise precepts – just like those he indited for his son Robert Cecil, Essex's enemy. Southampton had no good blood for his ancient guardian, who had died at last in 1598, so that it was safe to put something of him into Polonius.

Hamlet contains more about the theatre than do any of the other plays; this too reflected the contemporary situation. A sharp theatre warfare raged in those years, 1600–2, stirred up by Ben Jonson against Marston and Dekker. He attacked them in a couple of plays performed by the boys' company at Blackfriars; it blew up into a row between the private theatre of the boys' companies, and the public theatre of the men's. Shakespeare has several comments on it, including a good-tempered, 'Faith, there has been much to-do on both sides . . . O, there has been much throwing about of brains.' As for the boys, there is a bawdy pun: 'There is an eyrie of children, little eyases, that cry out on the top of the question and are most tyranically clapped for it. These are now the fashion, and so berattle the common stages – so they call them – that many . . . dare scarce come thither.' '*The common stages – so they call them*': there is the old contempt in which the profession had been held and which he had done so much to remedy, with perhaps a trace of his old resentment,

> That did not better for my life provide
> Than public means which public manners breeds.
> [*Sonnets*, CXI]

He goes on, 'who maintains 'em? Will they pursue the quality no longer than they can sing? Will they not say afterwards – as it is most like, if their means are no better – their writers do them wrong to make them exclaim against their own succession.' This means that their backers – mainly Jonson – do the boys an ill service, for when their voices break they will be glad enough to join the men's companies. It was the usual route for the boy actors, who sang and played women's parts. Meanwhile, the boys' companies were taking away custom. 'Do the boys carry it away?' 'Ay, that they do . . . Hercules and his load too', in other words the Globe's sign with Hercules carrying the globe. The Chamberlain's Men would certainly have to do something to meet the competition of the up-and-coming private theatre.

Hamlet also reveals, more than any other of his plays, Shakespeare's feeling about acting – the strangeness of the art, that an actor:

> Could force his soul so to his own conceit
> That from her working all his visage wanned,
> Tears in his eyes, distraction in's aspect,
> A broken voice, and his whole function suiting
> With forms to his conceit – and all for nothing!
> [*Hamlet*, II.ii.580]

We are given full insight, too, not only into his own view of acting but his practice as a producer. 'Speak the speech, I pray you, as I pronounced it to you, trippingly on the tongue', not mouth it like a town-crier, 'as many of our players do.' They were not to saw the air with their hand, but make their gestures smoothly. It offended him to the soul to hear a rumbustious, periwig-pated fellow tear a passion to tatters, 'to split the ears of the groundlings'. Though it might make the ignorant laugh, it made the judicious grieve.

He gives us his own recipe for good acting – discretion, though not too tame either: 'suit the action to the word, the word to the action'. Above all things be natural, for the purpose of playing, from the first to the last, 'was and is to hold, as 'twere, the mirror up to nature', and to express the very form and impact of the time. He had seen such bad acting in his experience,

Hamlet : title-page

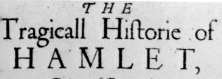

THE
Tragicall Historie of
HAMLET,
Prince of Denmarke.

By William Shakespeare.

Newly imprinted and enlarged to almost as much
againe as it was, according to the true and perfect
Coppie.

AT LONDON,
Printed by I. R. for N. L. and are to be sold at his
shoppe vnder Saint Dunstons Church in
Fleetstreet. 1604.

80

heard things so overdone – 'O there be players that I have seen play – and heard others praise, and that highly – that, neither having the accent of Christians, nor the gait of Christian, pagan, nor man, have so strutted and bellowed that I have thought some of Nature's journeymen had made men, and not made them well, they imitated humanity so abominably.'

Could anything be plainer? He deplored the uncouth prating and orating and stomping about the stage of the earlier Elizabethan drama, and himself stood for a more graceful and subtle style of acting – in keeping, we may observe, with his own nature. Observe, too, that this could be better provided for in the private theatre, with its smaller audience of a higher class, more intimate and more sophisticated. In the public theatre he had often seen clowns insert their own gags, not set down by the playwright, to make asses laugh, when it held up the necessary action of the piece; the clowns themselves starting the laugh 'to set on some quantity of barren spectators to laugh too. That's villainous, and shows a most pitiful ambition in the fool that uses it.' This is strong language; it shows too what he thought of the spectators. 'O, reform it altogether.'

By New Year 1601 Essex was coming to the end of his tether; he was drawing together around Essex House in the Strand his motley collection of adherents, young aristocrats, mostly swordsmen, young earls like Southampton and his friend Rutland; two Percys; the two Danvers brothers, who had been pardoned and returned from France; Lord Monteagle, who was to play a dubious part a few years later over the Gunpowder Plot; and many such irresponsibles. Essex, who had hovered long, was still undecided, until Southampton egged him on with, 'shall we resolve upon nothing then?'

The day before Essex's outbreak into the City a group of his followers crossed over to Bankside to see *Henry IV*. But, to put people in mind of the deposition of a monarch, they bribed the players to put on *Richard II*. Augustine Phillips said that, with an old play so much out of use, few would want to see it; however, he agreed to put it on, for an extra 40 shillings. It is a tribute to the actors' trained memory that they could perform it at such short notice. This was not only due to their theatrical expertise: all Elizabethan education was directed to training the memory – we see the most remarkable evidence of it in the magpie memory of the dramatist himself. All this circle were addicts of his work; we find one of the Percys writing that if he stayed longer in the country, at Dumbleton, 'at my return you will find me so dull that I shall be taken for Justice Silence or Justice Shallow'.

The rebellion was a complete fiasco, but it settled Essex's fate, along with several of his followers, including Sir Charles Danvers. Southampton had a narrow escape; he spoke up well at his trial and aroused much sympathy by his youthful appearance: he was now twenty-seven, old enough to know better. Great interest was made on his behalf to spare him; his mother wrote distractedly to Cecil blaming Essex for misleading her son and attributing his conduct to despair of ever winning the Queen's favour. She herself had displayed a royal courage at the crisis, but was furious at Essex's stealing her popularity: 'I am Richard II. Know ye not that? This tragedy was played forty times in open streets and houses.' Southampton disappeared, unrepentant, into the Tower to await a better day.

The Fall of Essex and Southampton

In the year 1601 there was published a garland of tributes to celebrate the long married happiness of Sir John Salusbury, Esquire of the Body to the Queen. (One of his family had been killed in the Essex affair, and another was to perish for his part in the Gunpowder Plot.) The tributes were written by the leading writers for the theatre, and Shakespeare contributed his exquisite poem, *The Phoenix and the Turtle*. Strangely enough, it is more of an elegiac poem, singing a requiem for the death and resurrection of love in the person of two chaste lovers, united in death, the emblem of one the royal phoenix, the other the humble dove, emblem of fidelity. What are we to think of:

> So they loved, as love in twain
> Had the essence but in one;
> Two distincts, division none. . . .
> [*The Phoenix and the Turtle*, 26]

when we remember, from the sonnets,

> Let me confess that we two must be twain,
> Although our undivided loves are one.
> [*Sonnets*, XXXVI]

There is the same sad beauty in *Twelfth Night* of this year, with its mingled atmosphere of melancholy, gaiety and music, and its magical songs. We are reminded of Shakespeare's exquisite response to music, and his genius as a song writer, all the way from the songs of *Two Gentlemen of Verona* to *The Tempest*. There is the nostalgic country charm of:

> When icicles hang by the wall,
> And Dick the shepherd blows his nail,
> And Tom bears logs into the hall,
> And milk comes frozen home in pail. . . .
> [*Love's Labour's Lost*, v.ii.922]

And,

> When all aloud the wind doth blow
> And coughing drowns the parson's saw –
> [*Love's Labour's Lost*, v.ii.931]

I always think of it in the large echoing church at Stratford. At the end, most magical of all, come 'Full fathom five thy father lies', and 'Fear no more the heat of the sun'. In Ariel's song,

> Come unto these yellow sands,
>   And then take hands,
> Curtsied when you have and kissed,
>   The wild waves whist. . . .
> [*The Tempest*, I.ii.376]

he is still remembering Marlowe, twenty years after, for the phrase, 'the wild waves whist', is his.

Now, in *Twelfth Night*, we have the lovely songs sung by Feste the Fool, 'O mistress mine, where are you roaming?', 'Come away, come away, death', and 'When that I was and a little tiny boy', on the tremulous verge between laughter and tears – like Mozart. And this is to say nothing of the bawdy songs of Ophelia's madness and others, the merry drinking songs, the snatches and catches of Autolycus and Sir Toby Belch. Here in *Twelfth Night* we have a snatch of song picked up the year before from Robert Jones's book of airs. We know the name of the player, Jack Wilson, who had sung 'Sigh no more, ladies'. O, what a genius Shakespeare had! No wonder all the world has always loved him.

The month before Essex's outbreak the Queen had a distinguished visitor from Italy, Valentino Orsino, Duke of Bracciano. The dramatist, on the alert for everything going and playing at Court at the time, picked up the names for his new comedy: Orsino for the Duke, Valentine for his gentleman. Many references show what a sensitive register he regularly was of everything to the fore. The Shirleys' account of their visit to the Sophy of Persia gets two mentions: 'the icicle on a Dutchman's beard' referred to Barentz' voyage into the Arctic at this time; Malvolio, his face wreathed with 'more lines than is in the new map with the augmentation of the Indies' ('augmentation' – how like his grand way with words!) refers to the new map with rhumb lines on the principles of projection, which had appeared the year before. We see how much this marvellous mind, with the retentive actor's memory, was *au fait* with everything, and poised to make use of it.

Similarly with *Troilus and Cressida* of the next year, 1602, into which went much of the disillusionment, the sickness at heart over the events of the past two or three years, the disenchantments of both war and love. Those are the very themes, and there is something new in him – a bitter, cynical realism in his treatment of them. A very different play again, it is one of the most remarkable he ever wrote – and one of the least popular: too near the bone. Its interest is highly intellectual; it has his most commanding thoughts on the absolute necessity of order and obedience, authority and duty, if any state is to prosper; in their absence, if they are not duly regarded or are undermined, society falls apart, and people suffer all the more in consequence. Shakespeare was sensitive about suffering and man's cruelty to man, unlike Marlowe: it was the authoritarian and upholder of social order who was the more humane spirit, not the moral anarchist, who didn't care.

All the same there were no illusions about human beings in his mind – no-one has ever understood them better. The treatment of love is even more disenchanted, Cressida a very whore (as Forman described Emilia). It is a mark of Shakespeare's universality that we can say of this play, along with the unfinished *Timon of Athens*, with much of *Hamlet* and *King Lear*, that they *include* Swift. This bitterness went against the grain: it was not in keeping with Shakespeare's normal nature. Still, there is nothing more embittering than to see one's friends deliberately court disaster, especially for such a man, whose nature was loyal, capable of warm friendship, but was not willing to run risks after will-o'-the-wisps.

He uses the specific words, 'fools on both sides', in this play, with the implication: a plague on both your houses! There are recognizable touches of Essex again:

> Things small as nothing, for request's sake only,
> He makes important.   [*Troilus and Cressida*, II.iii.179]

The Fall of Essex and Southampton

It had been his regular way with the Queen, a kind of emotional blackmail: intolerable. Something of the relationship between Essex and Southampton appears in that between the great Achilles and his young Patroclus: both sulking in their tents and contracting out of public life and duty when they could not get their way. Significantly enough, it is Shakespeare's only reference to a homosexual relationship in all his work – in glaring contrast with Marlowe, in whose work it is so prominent. Ben Jonson appears to have received a reproof in the Prologue, for later he riposted:

> Only amongst them, I am sorry for
> Some better natures, by the rest so drawn
> To run in that vile line.[2]

There we have him, always right as usual; but it exactly represents his attitude to Shakespeare: Ben couldn't resist him.

Silver Street, where Shakespeare lodged with the Mountjoys

WE KNOW PRECISELY where he was lodging in London at this time, 1602, and probably for some time before and after. We even have a depiction of

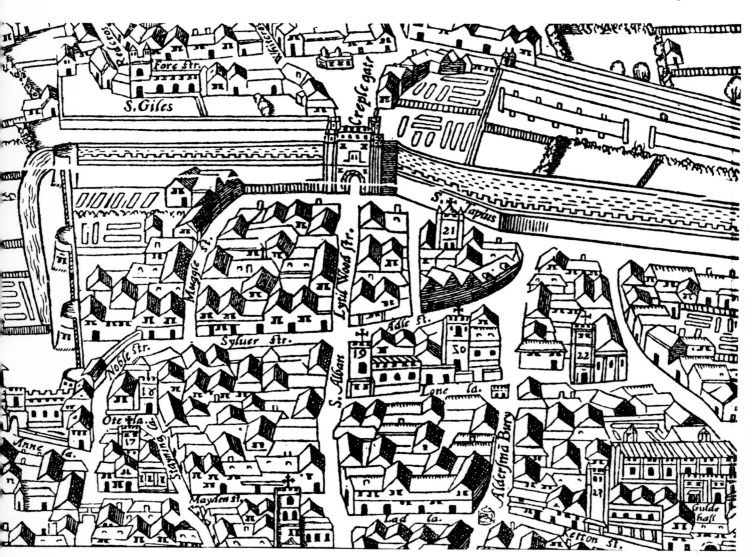

2 Ben Jonson, 'Apologetical Dialogue', q. E. K. Chambers, *William Shakespeare*, 11.205.

the house in Agas' map of London: twin gables and the pentice shop front at the corner of Silver Street and Mugle (or Monkswell) Street, within the north-west angle of the City Wall. Immediately outside the Wall was St Giles Cripplegate, where John Milton – who also could not resist the dramatist, for all his own chaste Puritanism – came to rest later in the century.

The pentice was the shop front of a French couple, the Mountjoys (Montjoie), tire-makers or headdress and periwig makers (we have noted his phrase 'periwig-pated'). The lodger was always addressed respectfully as 'Master' Shakespeare in the house, and regarded with confidence. Mrs Mountjoy pressed him to forward the marriage of her only daughter to her husband's apprentice, and Shakespeare actually performed the betrothal. The household was not a very godly one; the pious Huguenot church in London described both husband and son-in-law as *débauchés*, and Mrs Mountjoy was no better than she should be, as we know from the invaluable Simon Forman. What is more important to our purpose is that Shakespeare should have been lodging in this French household not long after writing the French scenes in *Henry V*, and perhaps at the time.

In March 1603 the Queen died. In spite of being called upon by a popular ballad to lament her, it was noticed that Shakespeare did not do so. He had paid tribute to her earlier, but the execution of Essex and the condemnation of Southampton were too bitter and too recent. Years would pass before he made his final salute to the glory of her reign in his last play, about her famous father, Henry VIII.

7

Jacobean Plays

WITH JAMES I'S ACCESSION Essex's followers were rehabilitated and in clover. Grants flowed fast and free. Southampton was released from the Tower, made Lord Lieutenant of his county, Keeper of the Isle of Wight, and given lucrative grants to console him for his troubles. With the privileged entry to the Privy Chamber it was rumoured that he might become the susceptible King's favourite; but at twenty-nine he was a little old for the part and not James's type. (He preferred more purely masculine types.) However, Southampton did for James what he had never done for Queen Elizabeth; he dropped his Catholicism and went to church. His mother received a handsome hand-out of the royal bounty.

The Chamberlain's Men shared in the generous new deal. Taken under James's patronage, they became the King's Men, their primacy acknowledged; the Admiral's Company became Prince Henry's, Worcester's the new Queen's. After the Presbyterian delights of Edinburgh neither James nor Anne could have enough of plays and masques. They wanted to see all the plays that they had not been able to see; performances at Court were doubled, and so was the rate of pay, from £10 under the provident Elizabeth to £20 under the improvident James. Money flowed in for Shakespeare and his Fellows.

The King's Men received special licence to play in any town or university; their leaders were given a status in the Royal Household as Grooms of the Chamber. As such Shakespeare and his Fellows received four and a half yards of scarlet cloth each for their liveries, to walk in procession on the King's reception by the City, and again next summer in that of the Spanish envoys sent to London to make the peace at last.

However, 1603 was again a bad plague year. The Court took to the country and in December was at Wilton where the King's Men presented three plays. Southampton was present – it is fascinating to think what former patron and poet would have had to say, after all that had passed. At

Court performances, including *Henry V* and *The Merchant of Venice*

The plaiers	On Twelfe Night	The poets
	We had a Maske before wth Ten drumes wth was Lyke to haue Come to Attend apon her ma no Trany in greate of dan wth a good defence wch they sett in wth excelent musike	
By his Ma:tis plaiers:	On the 7 of January was played the play off Henry the fift:	
By his Ma:tis plaiers :.	The 8 of January: A play Cauled Euery on out of his vmor	
By his Ma:tis plaiers :.	On Candelmas night A play Euery one Jn his vmor	
	The Sunday ffollowing A playe prouided And discharged	
By his Ma:tis plaiers:	On Shrousunday A play off the Marthant of venis	Shaxberd
By his Ma:tis plaiers :.	On Shroumonday A Tragidie of the Spanishe Maz:	
By his Ma:tis players :.	On Shroutusday A play Cauled The Martchant of venis Againe Comanded By the Kings Ma:tie :.	Shaxberd:

Christmas the Company was playing at Hampton Court and Whitehall, and were well paid for the cancellation of performances owing to the plague. Their performances at Court jumped to more than a dozen a year, more than all other companies combined; it was becoming a larger source of profit than the Globe itself. This had its effect upon the skilful, flexible dramatist in devising, or revising, plays and performances; he had to keep both types of audience in view, the character of his plays changing in accordance.

By the time of the King of Denmark's visit to his sister, James's Queen, in 1606, we find a Court official reporting, 'Burbage is come and says there is no new play the Queen has not seen, but they have revived an old one called *Love's Labour's Lost*, which for wit and mirth will please her exceedingly. And this is appointed to be played tomorrow at my Lord of Southampton's ... Burbage is my messenger.' This shows the familiar terms upon which the King's Men were with Court officials, and we know the special interest this play had had for Southampton and his circle. It was to be performed at Southampton House, for which it had been originally directed.

Shakespeare's next play, *All's Well that Ends Well*, is again something different; works of genius often fit into no precise category, and this and its successor, *Measure for Measure*, are sometimes labelled bitter comedies. We know what little regard Shakespeare had for labelling plays, from the fun he poked at it in *Hamlet*. Both these plays continue the disenchanted comment on the times so marked in *Troilus and Cressida*. A recent editor of *All's Well* has noticed that Shakespeare drew much more on his experience of the world around him than people without a knowledge of that world realize. But of course – real writers do; it is only that Shakespeare's work has been submerged under mountains of academic commentary without any sense of the life of the time.

These plays, in fact, have a strong element of coarse Jacobean realism. Parolles, the braggart coward of a soldier, has nothing of the inner joyousness of Falstaff; he is drawn from without, really a Jonsonian type – a tribute to the influence of the junior upon his senior, who from the beginning to the end was willing to learn from anyone, to pick up tips from anywhere. The characters from low life in *Measure for Measure* are very convincing and nasty – Shakespeare knew them well enough from living alone in London: Mistress Overdone, the brothel madam, her pimp Pompey, the condemned prisoner and the horrid executioner, Abhorson, Lucio the dissolute young waster of a gentleman – there were plenty of them about in Jacobean society grown extravagant and spendthrift. We are in a different world from the joyous bawdry of the Boar's Head in East Cheap; there is a touch of sourness in the merriment, and even in the subjects.

All's Well presents a petulant young aristocrat, spirited but spoiled, who refuses to be tied down in marriage and turns up his nose at the admirable girl, beneath him socially, who loves him. His mother, however, kind and good, is sympathetic to the girl and wants him to marry her. There is a new note in the play; earlier, Shakespeare had been glamourized by his admission into the world of a young earl. Experience had taught him that *there* were as great fools as anywhere else. He had always reserved his own independence, and as a player had been in a fortunate position to observe it all without being

Queen Elizabeth in State

Clemens et Regni moderatrix iusta Britāni
Hac forma insigni conspicienda nitet.

Tristia dum gentes circùm omnes bella fatigant,
Cæciq; errores toto grassantur in orbe.
An. Dñi. pace beas longa, verâ et pietate Britannos: 1579
Iusticia moderans miti sapienter habenas.
Chara domi, celebrisq; foris, longæuaq; regnū
Hic teneas, regno tandem fruitura perenni.

LEFT King James I, who became patron of Shakespeare's Company RIGHT James I's queen, Anne of Denmark, who much appreciated Shakespeare's plays

committed – *engagé* in our contemporary *cliché*. Here is his new comment:

Honours thrive
When rather from our acts we them derive
Than our foregoers – 　[*All's Well That Ends Well*, II.iii.142]

i.e. ancestors and all that, by which society set so much store, and quarrelled on the silly subject. Even Parolles was more sensible:

Simply the thing I am
Shall make me live – 　[*All's Well That Ends Well*, IV.iii.369]

a better recipe in the struggle for survival.

For *Measure for Measure* we see Shakespeare turning over several versions of the story to see which would make the best drama. He toned down several of the original Italian features to make it more tolerable, where later Jacobean dramatists would have accentuated them, and turned the play into the lurid melodrama of a dramaturgy in decadence, and a public out for mere sensationalism. The play was written in 1604; it has a sympathetic reference to the new King's dislike of crowds and popular clamour (in contrast to the great actress with such an instinct for playing to the gallery). For the coronation in March Jonson and other dramatists wrote devices; Shakespeare was too busy – we see how pressed with work he was, having to depute taking possession of his land at Stratford to his brother and handing over the farming of his tithes to an agent.

All's Well was performed at Court at Christmas; but his second play of this year, *Othello, the Moor of Venice*, had been performed on Hallowmas Day, 1 November, in the banqueting house at Whitehall (the old wooden one, not the present building shortly to be built by Ben Jonson's colleague and competitor in Court masques, Inigo Jones). The Company had been on tour that autumn, visiting Dover – so the celebrated description of Shakespeare's Cliff in the play shortly to be written is authenticated:

> How fearful
> And dizzy 'tis to cast one's eye so low!
> The crows and choughs that wing the midway air
> Show scarce so gross as beetles. Half-way down
> Hangs one that gathers samphire, dreadful trade!
> [*King Lear*, IV.vi.12]

– the Elizabethans used samphire in cooking –

> The fishermen that walk upon the beach
> Appear like mice, and yond tall anchoring bark
> Diminished to her cock, her cock a buoy
> Almost too small for sight. The murmuring surge,
> That on the unnumbered idle pebbles chafes,
> Cannot be heard so high.   [*King Lear*, IV.vi.17]

In the summer of 1604 James had visited Oxford, and been received with Three Sibyls saluting Banquo; it is thought that these reappear, in the imagination of the dramatist, in the Three Weird Sisters who appear to

The palace of Whitehall

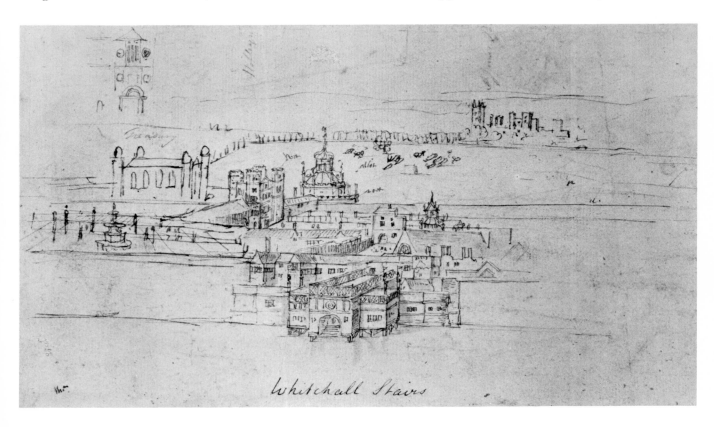

Whitehall Stairs

GLOBE. SOUTHWARKE.

" our theaters are wasted downe
and where they stoode scarce septupled
by wyves of tombe maye
and midwyves of te owre

LEFT The Globe Theatre
ABOVE The Chandos portrait
of William Shakespeare

ABOVE Macbeth from
Holinshed's *Chronicles*

OPPOSITE *King Lear*, performed
at Court before James I,
who took over the patronage of
the Chamberlain's Company.

Macbeth and James's putative ancestor, Banquo, in the play shortly to be
written and closely associated with the Scottish king. It is clear, over and
over, that with this writer all was grist that came to his mill.

Othello is an inspired play, written straightforwardly in one swift rush of
the imagination; the theme and colouring appealed to the romantic that was
so characteristic of Shakespeare – in contrast to Jonson – so that we have a
depiction like a Tintoretto or a Veronese, the language rich as their
Renaissance paint. In this play, and in *Antony and Cleopatra*, the language
itself reaches heights and depths never reached before, and never excelled
since:

> Not poppy, nor mandragora,
> Nor all the drowsy syrups of the world –
> [*Othello*, III.iii.330]

The heart turns over hearing it –

> The odds is gone,
> And there is nothing left remarkable
> Beneath the visiting moon.
> [*Antony and Cleopatra*, IV.xiii.65]

With *King Lear* of 1605 – in which the description of the dizzy cliff at
Dover appears, shortly after the Company's visit – the exploring mind of
their dramatist seeks new territory to conquer, with the pre-history of
Britain. The Elizabethans did not distinguish it clearly from recorded
history. Like the reading man he was, Shakespeare looked up the historians
Holinshed and Camden, and took up anything else that was useful, from

94

M. William Shak-ſpeare:

HIS
True Chronicle Hiſtorie of the life and
death of King LEAR and his three
Daughters.

With the vnfortunate life of Edgar, ſonne
and heire to the Earle of Gloſter, and his
ſullen and aſſumed humor of
TOM of Bedlam:

as it was played before the Kings ~~Maieſtie~~ *at Whitehall*
~~S.~~ *Stephans night in Chriſtmas* ~~Hollidayes.~~

By his Maieſties ſeruants playing vſually at the Gloabe
on the Bancke-ſide.

LONDON,
Printed for *Nathaniel Butter*, and are to be ſold at his ſhop in *Pauls*
Church-yard at the ſigne of the Pide Bull neere
St. *Auſtins* Gate. 1608.

IVDICIO PYLIVM GENIO SOCRATEM ARTE MARONEM
TERRA TEGIT POPVLVS MÆRET OLYMPVS HABET

STAY PASSENGER WHY GOEST THOV BY SO
READ IF THOV CANST WHOM ENVIOVS
WITH IN THIS MONVMENT SHAKSPEARE WE WHOM

Richard Carew, Sidney and Spenser. The names of the crazy fiends come from Harsnet's exposure of recent claims of Catholic priests to exorcize demons from hysterical women, exorcism appealing to fools as much then as today.[1]

What is odd is this. In other versions of the old story, King Lear does not go mad. However, a year or two before the play was written, a gentleman-pensioner of the Queen, Sir Brian Annesley, was certified as insane by two grasping elder daughters after his inheritance. His youngest daughter, Cordell or Cordelia, tried to protect him. Three years after the play, in 1608, she married the young widower of Southampton's mother, Sir William Harvey.

Everyone has noticed the sick mood in which Shakespeare refers to sex in these plays, or, rather, with sex as a sickness, from *Hamlet* and *Troilus and Cressida* to *King Lear*. Now, in this, we get:

> Adultery?
> Thou shalt not die: die for adultery! No.
> [*King Lear*, IV.vi.112]

In the sonnets he had made no bones about being an adulterer himself, and so was his married mistress, Emilia Lanier. In *Othello* Emilia – that name again! – had no objection to it. Now,

> The fitchew [polecat], nor the soiled horse, goes to 't
> With a more riotous appetite.
> Down from the waist they are centaurs,
> Though women all above.   [*King Lear*, IV.vi.124]

Though no-one wrote more affectingly of the young and innocent, Ophelia and Desdemona, Perdita and Marina, no-one wrote more scathingly of women without innocence.

Macbeth followed in 1606, inspired by the great event of the autumn before, the Gunpowder Plot, and full of references to it. It was written to pay tribute to the King, with its commendation of Banquo, his legendary ancestor. There had been a surge of popularity for the new royal house on their deliverance, which the dramatist was quick to take advantage of. Banquo, the witches foretell, though not a king himself, shall be the ancestor of kings; he is given attributes that would be music to James's ears, very susceptible to flattery: his 'royalty of nature', the 'dauntless temper of his mind', the 'wisdom that doth guide his valour'. Shakespeare was never one to miss a point (unlike the professors who talk about his 'transmuting' experience of what went on around him and cannot even *see* a point).

James's well-known interest in witches and demonology is catered for: he had written a book on the subject in Scotland. There are further tributes to his powers, as an anointed king, of healing the King's Evil; it is hinted, not obscurely, that His Majesty spoke with the afflatus of inspiration. His best quality, his desire to bring about a general peace throughout Europe and to appear before the world as *rex pacificus*, is acclaimed.

There are several references to the Gunpowder Plot. At the trial of the conspirators the Jesuit Provincial, Garnet, confessed that he had learned of it

Shakespeare's bust looks down on his grave at Stratford

[1] cf. my *The Elizabethan Renaissance: The Life of the Society*, Chapter 9.

EYGENTLICHE ABBILDVNG WIE ETTLICH ENGLISCHE EDELLEVT EINE
schließen den König sampt dem gantzen Parlament mit Pulfer zuuertilgen.

Ein Spruchwort ist vô alters gsehe
Ein Kräh sich zu der andern gsellt
Solchs sicht man hie auff diesem Blatt
Das sich ein Rott versamblet hatt
Etlich Englischer Edellout
Zuthun das Gott höchlich verbeut.
Der Ruhrfinck Robert Catesby
Der ander war Thomas Percy,
Allbeide von edlem geschlecht,
So man daselbst nennet Schilt knecht
Diese brachten noch mehr ins Spiel
wie wol es war ihr eigen will,
Dann wer gern dantzt dē ist gar gut
Pfeiffen, das er bals springen thut
Robert winter walte nicht seyn
Der letzt, bracht auch vnd sich binei
Sein Bruder in solch hellisch verbund
Jobn vnd Christoffdright zur fü
ihrn willen theten auch ergeben,
welchs sie heut Koster ihr leben.
Robert Bates sein Herrn getreuw
wolt seyn, welch ehn hernach gereuw
Der beste Mann (meyns bunderseh)
war Guido Faukes, welcher sich
Anzuzünden hat Vnternommen
Das Fewr hernach stel noch kommē
In dieser Gsellschafft, Digby, Grant,
Rockwoud, Keyes vnd vngenant.
                                    Ihr

Robert
winter | Christopher
wright | John
wright | Thomas
Percy | Guido
Fawkes | Robert
Catesby

Bates

Abbildung wie vnd welcher gestalt ettliche der furnemsten Verrahter in Engellant von Leben zum tod hin

Conspiran Angli, moliti perede regem,
    Et regnum, peraunt sequi caputq, suum.
Supplicium specta, lector, miraber, mi vllum
    Si pectus sceleris tanta libido cadat

Anno. 1606.
Meuæ. Feb.

Voicy (amy lecteur) comme les conspirateurs contre le Roy D'an
ilz ont esté traine sur vn matras au lieu du supplice, et pendus a vne
mis sur vn banc, et ouuert le ventre, et leurs ictez le coeur a la face,
en haulteur et les testes mis sur des perces de fer, et les entreilles br

Gunpowder Plot

98

beforehand, but under the seal of confession. By the Jesuit doctrine of equivocation he need not tell the truth under examination, merely 'equivocate', i.e. lie. The word caught the popular fancy; Shakespeare as usual expressed the popular view. What was an equivocator? One that 'could swear in both scales against either scale, who committed treason enough for God's sake, yet could not equivocate to heaven'. 'What is a traitor?' asks the boy Macduff. 'Why, one that swears and lies ... Every one that does so is a traitor, and must be hanged.' The Jesuit Provincial was hanged; Shakespeare would no more have regretted it than his countrymen at large.

The dramatist was thinking of his next play before he had finished *Macbeth*; for Macbeth says of Banquo:

> under him
> My genius is rebuked; as, it is said,
> Mark Antony's was by Caesar [i.e. Augustus].
> [*Macbeth*, III.i.57]

Antony and Cleopatra was written in 1607, when Daniel put out a revised edition of his *Cleopatra*, profiting from Shakespeare's play. There was a certain kinship of spirit between these two writers; both of them men of the people, who had had little enough to support their arduous beginnings (though Daniel had been at Oxford); both of them independent-spirited, but courteous and gentlemanly.

Though the subject of the play was a great love story, it is noticeably touched with irony and disillusion: the world is not well lost for love, and it is the cool politician – as it might be a Cecil – who inherits the earth. And the action of the play, as a descendant of the Cecils has seen, is more concerned with the faction-fighting of the age, partisan and party warfare. Shakespeare continues his disillusioned comment on it; he had seen Essex's followers slip away at his fall – Francis Bacon even before it – and recruit themselves to Cecil:

> The hearts
> That spanieled me at heels, to whom I gave
> Their wishes, do discandy, melt their sweets
> On blossoming Caesar. [*Antony and Cleopatra*, IV.xii.21]

There are the familiar strictures on the people and their incapacity to judge anything or anybody:

> our slippery people,
> Whose love is never linked to the deserver
> Till his deserts are past. [*Antony and Cleopatra*, I.ii.192]

As for their judgment:

> I see men's judgments are
> A parcel of their fortunes – [*Antony and Cleopatra*, III.xiii.31]

and go up and down with them, incapable of any objectivity or justice of mind.

The play was fairly clearly written at home in Stratford, for it is full of country images and has a good deal of quiet reading in it. Moreover, it has elaborate stage directions, with notes for position, movements and even gestures, for others producing the play in his absence. In the summer of 1607, when Shakespeare went to the country, his intelligent elder daughter, Susanna, married a doctor, John Hall, a Cambridge man, who became a well-known practitioner among the country gentry of Warwickshire. He prescribed for Shakespeare's fellow-Warwickshireman, Michael Drayton, who spent his summers with the Rainsfords at Clifford Chambers, just across the fields from Stratford. In the summer of next year, 1608, the gentleman of New Place sued John Addenbrooke for a debt of £6. Since he did not pay up, Shakespeare sued his surety in Stratford. Another suitor in court that year had the romantic name of Florizel, which the dramatist picked up for use in a future play – the prince in *The Winter's Tale*. That autumn his mother, Mary Arden, died; while he was called out to be godfather to the child of Alderman Walker, baptized William after him. He remembered him in his will.

Besides North's *Plutarch* he looked up Livy, in Philemon Holland's translation – published a few years before, in 1600. He adapted a useful fable from Camden's recent *Remains Concerning Britain*, out in 1605; and used hints from *Four Paradoxes or Political Discourses*, propounding the martial virtues as against the ill humours of peace, by Thomas Digges, out in 1604. We see how much Shakespeare kept in touch with the new books appearing, and what use he made of them. The Diggeses were acquaintances, one of them a stepson of Sir Thomas Russell, who lived out at leafy Alderminster, a few miles from Stratford, and whom Shakespeare nominated overseer of his will; another Digges contributed well-known memorial verses to the First Folio and the *Poems* put out in 1640.

The winter of 1607–8 was excessively cold; the Thames froze over and coals of fire were burned in the fun-fair upon the ice. This appears as: 'the coal of fire upon the ice'. Next year Ben Jonson scoffed at a rather silly line of the master's:

> He lurched all swords of the garland.
> [*Coriolanus*, II.ii.105]

In *Epicoene, or The Silent Woman*, Ben improved on this: 'You have lurched your friends of the better half of the garland.'

The long struggle with Spain had had a unifying effect upon the nation, intensifying its patriotism. Now that pressure was relaxed with the peace, things were falling apart; class feeling was sharpened by the extravagance and ostentation of the Jacobean court, which set no such example to the nation as had the great Queen. To these griefs were added a sharp dearth of corn, always dangerous when people lived near subsistence level, and popular resentment against enclosures of arable by the gentry. There were disturbances in Northamptonshire in 1607, which spread to Warwickshire. William Combe wrote to Cecil reporting the troubles. Shakespeare was now a Warwickshire landlord like Combe.

In his forthcoming play, *Coriolanus*, he concentrated much of the action on just these issues: the dearth of corn, class conflict, the pros and cons of peace or war, all beating against the rock-like figure of a war hero who cannot adapt himself to the politics of peace, let alone the *demos* and democratic humbug. *Some* humbug is necessary in society to cement it together, and Coriolanus is wrong not to make concessions to it. Shakespeare gave a more favourable picture of the war-hero than was the historical fact, for his own purposes, with the most unfavourable depiction of the mob and the utter hopelessness of a society where direction has broken down:

> where gentry, title, wisdom
> Cannot conclude but by the yea or no
> Of general ignorance, it must omit
> Real necessities.   [*Coriolanus*, III.i.144]

'Nothing is done to purpose' – how true that is we see today in democratic society breaking down all round us. This most perceptive commentator on society points a finger to the truth, no less than Swift:

> And manhood is called foolery when it stands
> Against a falling fabric.   [*Coriolanus*, III.i.247]

8

Last Years

THE DECISIVE INFLUENCE of the social conditions of the time is brought home to us by the effects of the plague, which reigned again severely during 1608–9 and shut most of the theatres for nearly a year and a half. Once more theatres, printers, publishers and writers were affected, as in 1592–3, though not the companies which were now too strongly established. But something of the effects is observable in Shakespeare's work. The play that was next in his mind, *Timon of Athens*, was left unfinished; *Pericles*, which was notably successful when the theatres could open, was never published in its proper form, as Edward Blount (Marlowe's friend and publisher) intended. The proper copy seems to have been lost, and the play has come down to us in a mangled form. Heming and Condell even excluded it from their collection of their Fellow's work.

The interest of *Timon of Athens* to us is precisely its unfinishedness, for it reveals to us how Shakespeare wrote his plays. Dramatist first and last, he visualized his scenes separately and wrote them up, not necessarily following the straightforward development of the plot as a modern writer would. It is fascinating to watch the scenes taking shape in his mind, chunks of prose intermingled with epigrammatic rhymed couplets just as they occurred to him.

While reading North's *Plutarch* for *Coriolanus* he noted the stories of Timon and Alcibiades, as usual, for the next play. This is full of *désabusé* comments on contemporary society, which seems to have displeased him as much as it did Drayton. Indeed there was much that was displeasing in Jacobean society to those who had known the ardours and endurances of the high Elizabethan age and who had come to maturity in the heroic Armada days. (As for those today who graduated in the heroic days of 1940–5.)

At the apex of society James and Anne set poor examples, both of them rather drunken and extravagant, he homosexual in his tastes, she featherheaded and silly, neither of them at all dignified. There was the vulgar

Stratford's Holy Trinity Church, where Shakespeare is buried ostentation, the sycophancy and flattery, the pretences and humbug about art and letters (James and Anne cared little for either), the more sordid aspects of a society on the make. A sad decline of standards was evident, with relaxation at the top – shortly to erupt in the appalling scandal of the murder of Sir Thomas Overbury, the father of the poisoner being James's Lord Treasurer who made a fortune out of embezzling from the state.

Much of this kind of thing is in the play; and a main theme of it is the gold craze in Virginia. Jamestown had been founded the year before, in 1607; instead of cultivating the soil and laying up stocks in order to survive, the colonists wasted their time digging for gold. The report came back, 'no talk, no hope, no work but to dig gold, wash gold, refine gold, load gold'. There

The Virginia Colony

The arriual of the Englishemen in Virginia.	II.

The sea coasts of Virginia arre full of Ilāds, wehr by the entrance into the mayne lād is hard to finde. For although they bee separated with diuers and sundrie large Diuision, which seeme to yeeld conuenient entrance, yet to our great perill we proued that they wear shallowe, and full of dangerous flatts, and could neuer perce opp into the mayne lād, vntill wee made trialls in many places with or small pinnesſ. At lengthe wee fownd an entrance vppon our mens diligent serche therof. After that wee had paſſed opp, and ſayled ther in for aſhort ſpace we diſcouered a migthye riuer fallnige downe in to the ſownde ouer againſt thoſe Ilands, which neuertheleſſe wee could not ſaile opp any thinge far by Reaſon of the ſhallewnes, the mouth ther of beinge annoyed with ſands driuen in with the tyde therfore ſaylinge further, wee came vnto a Good bigg yland, the Inhabitante therof as ſoone as they ſaw vs began to make a great an horrible crye, as people which meuer befoer had ſeene men apparelled like vs, and camme a way makinge out crys like wild beaſts or men out of their wyts. But beenge gentlye called backe, wee offred the of our wares, as glaſſes, kniues, babies, and other trifles, which wee thougt they dcligted in. Soe they ſtood ſtill, and perceuinge our Good will and courteſie came fawninge vppon vs, and bade us welcome. Then they brougt vs to their village in the iland called, Roanoac, and vnto their Weroans or Prince, which entertained vs with Reaſonable curteſie, althoug the wear amaſed at the firſt ſight of vs. Suche was our arriuall into the parte of the world, which we call Virginia, the ſtature of bodee of wich people, theyr attire, and maneer of lyuinge, their feaſts, and banketts, I will particullerlye declare vnto yow.

was no gold, and the fools starved. It is all made use of in Timon's search for gold and having to subsist on roots.

So far from William Shakespeare not being in touch with what was going on in the world around him, 'transcending' experience, 'transmuting' it – this kind of academicism really reflects ignorance of the time and circumstances. He himself has told us what the case was: the theatre and the players are 'the abstract and brief chronicles of the time'.

In 1607, too, appeared Twyne's *The Pattern of Painful Adventures* which suggested the subject of *Pericles*; the fantastic story of Apollonius of Tyre was much in the air just then, and Shakespeare caught at it. He also read up John Gower, as he had done Chaucer for *A Midsummer Night's Dream*, and made use of Gower as a chorus to bring the disparate events together, as he had done in *Henry V*. The play was very successful when put on; a pamphlet of 1609 says,

> Amazed I stood to see a crowd . . .
> So that I truly thought all these
> Came to see *Shore* or *Pericles*.[1]

Jonson wrote grumpily about a play so fadged up:

> No doubt some mouldy tale
> Like *Pericles* . . .
> May keep up the Play-club.[2]

The brothel scenes, which are such a feature of it, would appeal highly to an Elizabethan audience. The virtuous Victorians liked to think these were not by their author – they were apt to put their writers on pedestals. On the contrary, these scenes are just like him, and the bawdy is the natural bawdy of a highly sexed heterosexual; he toned down the incest theme in the original, and we now realize clearly that there was nothing homosexual or even ambivalent about him.

The popularity of the play was cashed in on by several writers. We need only notice George Wilkins' novel, *The Painful Adventures of Pericles Prince of Tyre*; for we now know that he kept a shady inn at which lodged the young couple, the Mountjoys' daughter and son-in-law, whom Shakespeare had betrothed. Here is a new link.[3] These two years of disarray affected publishers and printers no less than the theatre. 'Plays were rushed to the printers by needy playwrights . . . the temptation of piracy must have been especially great for the unemployed minor dramatist, actor, or [theatre] bookkeeper.' A minor publisher, one Gosson, rushed out a surreptitious version of the play in these conditions: hence the unsatisfactory text we have of it.

A much more important manuscript was acquired, in these conditions at this time, by a reputable and exceptional publisher, Thomas Thorpe. He was a friend of Edward Blount, of literary inclinations, and given to flowery dedications. He had acquired a complete collection of Shakespeare's sonnets, of those earlier plague years, and was effusively grateful to the Mr W.H., the only person who had them – we are even more so. It was always obvious that the person who held them would be someone close to Southampton, and

---

[1] *Pimlico, or Run Redcap*, anonymous.
[2] Ben Jonson, 'Ode to Himself', q. E.K.Chambers, *William Shakespeare*, II.210.
[3] Which we owe to the perceptive scholarship of Mr Roger Prior.

indeed there came out of the same *cache A Lover's Complaint*, Shakespeare's prentice piece for the young Earl's favour. What has created so much unnecessary confusion is quite familiar knowledge to an historian of the time: it was regular usage to address a knight as Mr, as in 'Mr W. H.', but totally out of the question for a lord.

The *Sonnets* were published in this year 1609, years after the story they relate. Southampton's mother had died in 1607, leaving all her household goods and chattels to her husband, Sir William Harvey. He was still a youngish man, and next year, 1608, married a young wife; this is why Thorpe wishes him 'all happiness' and 'that eternity promised by our ever-living poet' – which was what the poet had promised his young patron years before, if only he would marry and perpetuate himself in his progeny. 'Ever-living' is Thorpe's way of referring to Shakespeare still alive; 'wisheth the well-wishing adventurer in setting forth, T. T.' is another flowery way of alluding to the Adventurers in the Virginia Company of this year, 1609, among which Southampton appeared in the lead. (He was in time to become Treasurer of the Company.)

That is the common sense of the matter. But T. T.'s literary floweriness has given rise to whole libraries of confused conjecture and pointless 'theories'.

Just as out of the disarray of the plague years 1592–3 there emerged the Lord Chamberlain's Company, so now in 1608–9 there emerged a most important new step: taking over the private theatre in Blackfriars. It may well be that the intermission from playing gave them the opportunity to discuss and plan the move, for it needed careful consideration. If it succeeded, it would gain several ends; it would extinguish the rivalry of the boys' company there, provide a theatre for indoor, winter performances, in the evenings by candlelight, not only by day; with a more select and expensive audience it would yield larger profits – if it succeeded. That depended a good deal on the Company's dramatist, for it would need a rather new kind of play, at the same time as he would continue to provide fare for the Globe. Here was another challenge for the flexibly-minded playwright, ready to turn his hand to anything.

The new theatre, with its smaller space and select audience, demanded quieter, more intimate acting, with more music and elaborate staging, the element of the masque to the fore. This fitted in with the taste of the Court, with its fashion for masques; performances at Court and at Blackfriars would become more important and more profitable to the King's Men. The Company was in a stage of transition; this is clearly reflected in the plays that their dramatist would provide them with – the last phase in his writing.

The Burbages already owned the Blackfriars theatre, but had been leasing it out. In the summer of 1608 they made arrangements to take it over and run it on a co-operative basis. They bought the lease back and, to finance the new venture, they formed a group within the King's Men to put down capital and share the rent. The members were Shakespeare, Heming, Condell and Sly, with the Burbages, and Evans who had been directing the boys there. We see what an exceptional incentive this gave; the leading Fellows were part-owners and were already part-sharers at the Globe. Heming and Condell

Simon Forman's account of *Cymbeline*, which he saw acted at the Globe

of Cimbalin king of England

Remember also the storri of Cymbalin king
of England in Lucius tyme. howe Lucius
cam from octauus Cesar for Tribut and
being denied. after sent Lucius to a gretat
Armi of Soulddiars who landed at milfard
hauen. and After wer vanquished by Cimbalin and Lucius taken prisoner and all
by meanes of 3 outlawes of the which 2 of them
were the sonns of Cimbalin stolen from
him when they were but 2 yers old. by an
old man whom Cimbalin banished. and
he kept them as his own sonns 20 yers w
him in A cave. And howe on of them slew
Cloten that was the quens sonne goinge
To milford hauen to sek the loue of Innogen
the kinge daughter whom he had banished also
for louinge his daughter. and howe the Italian
that cam from her loue conveied him selfe
into A Cheste. and said yt was a chest of plate
sent from her loue & others to be presented to th
kinge. And in the depth of the night she being
a slepe. he opened the cheste & cam forth
of yt. And vewed her in her bed and the
markes of her body. & toke a way her braslet
& after Accused her of adultery to her loue &c
And in thend howe he cam to thend thes domings into
England c was taken prisoner and after reveled
to Innogen. who had turned her self
into mans apparell & fled to mek her
loue at milford hauen & chanchsed to
fall on the Caue in the wodde wher her 2
brothers were & howe by eating a sleping
Dram they thought she had bine deed & laid
her in the woode & the body of cloten by her.
in her loues apparell that he left behind him
& howe she was found by Lucius &c

were able to buy property in London, as Shakespeare had done at Stratford. Five years later he bought himself the gatehouse at Blackfriars; very convenient for winter residence, and another substantial investment. One of the sureties for this property was the landlord of the Mermaid – so another old tradition receives corroboration to this extent. It is Thomas Fuller of the *Worthies* who tells us of the 'wit-combats' there between Shakespeare and Ben Jonson, probable enough anyway.

With the return to normal, but for new conditions, Shakespeare wrote *Cymbeline*. What is striking for our purpose is that it is not only experimental but full of reminiscences of his earlier work – he had been re-reading it. The motivation of the play is that of *The Rape of Lucrece*, a husband's wager as to his wife's chastity during his absence; there are references going back to *Lucrece*, and earlier to *Titus Andronicus*; Imogen is described as 'the rare Arabian bird' of *The Phoenix and the Turtle*.

His next play, *The Winter's Tale*, was probably written at home in the winter and spring of 1610–11 – he was taking things more easily now, writing only one play a year against his previous average of two. This is more full of country atmosphere and activities than any of his plays since *A Midsummer Night's Dream*. We are given meads and pastures and un-numbered flowers, country folk and their junketings, a sheep-shearing feast with its folk-songs, and the pedlar Autolycus. The writer is at home, at Stratford. It is amusing that he turned to an early romance of Greene for his story, and used it up to the hilt – numerous echoes occur from it; and not only from Greene's tale of *Pandosto* but from his cony-catching pamphlets, with their pickpockets and tricksters, his transcripts from the low life he knew so well, for Greene had lived it, unlike the player he had known with his gentlemanly airs and confidence in himself. Really, if poor Greene could see the transformation effected, he would turn in his grave!

THE PLANTING OF ENGLISH STOCK in Virginia, the founding of the first English colony in the New World, aroused mounting interest in these years. In 1602, with time on his hands in the Tower, Southampton backed a voyage to explore the New England coast for a suitable settlement; in 1605 he fitted out another voyage there. Later he became interested in the southern area, where Hampton Roads, Hampton River and the original Southampton Hundred were named for him. The second Virginia Charter of 1609, with its roll-call of adventurers (i.e. investors), the phrase taken up by Thorpe, provided the big impulse and the wherewithal for settlement. Southampton and nearly 600 people subscribed, and lost; the prudent dramatist invested nothing, only in Stratford and Blackfriars.

The grand effort enabled a fleet to set sail complete with colonists; but they met with a tempest that sounds like a tornado. The flagship, the *Sea Venture*, ran on the rocks of Bermuda and broke up, though not a life was lost. On the uninhabited island the colonists remained for months, until they had constructed pinnaces in which they reached Virginia in the spring. They had sufficient to eat – wild hogs, fish and game; but the isle was supposed to be haunted, full of noises, which the shipwrecked attributed to spirits and devils.

William Strachey, who had gone out as Secretary to the colony – a job the poet Donne had wanted – sent home a newsletter describing their extraordinary experiences. Strachey was interested in literature and in the theatre; regularly in and out of Blackfriars, he had been a shareholder in the boys' company who had been acting there, and he contributed a sonnet to Jonson's *Sejanus* on its publication. Various acquaintances of Shakespeare, besides Southampton, were interested in Virginia, notably Sir Dudley Digges, who was also a friend and neighbour of both Heming and Condell. Sir Dudley possessed a portrait of the Danish astronomer, Tycho Brahe, with the names of his ancestors, Rosencrantz and Guildenstern, on it.

Shakespeare pounced on Strachey's newsletter in his usual manner, missing nothing; the subject appealed more than usually to his imagination. Out of it came his penultimate play, one of the finest of all, *The Tempest*, with its magical atmosphere of an enchanted isle, full of noises and spirits, the sojourn there like a primitive commonwealth. He got from Strachey the phenomenon of St Elmo's fire running down the rigging; Strachey mentions the description of the islands by Gonzalo Ferdinando Oviedo, whose first names were used for characters. Shakespeare was a reader of Hakluyt's *Voyages*, and of others such as Richard Eden. He had read Montaigne's essay on cannibals – John Florio had translated the *Essays* and Edward Blount published them in 1603. Gonzalo's description of a commonwealth, holding all things in common, comes from this source.

> All things in common nature should produce
> Without sweat or endeavour . . .
> No marrying? –
> None, man; all idle; whores and knaves.
> [*The Tempest*, ii.i.159]

Such was the brisk comment of this practical man, who knew what hard work was and had had a long struggle of it, whom no amount of imagination could seduce from common sense. He knew that in such a commonwealth no-one would work – that was the case in Virginia: they starved, and died.[4] The chief imaginative creation of the play, Caliban, was of course a play on the word cannibal, and it provided Shakespeare's comment on illusions about the goodness of primitive human nature. No one has ever known better the facts about human nature in the round.

The play was written later than the spring of 1611, when Simon Forman saw *The Winter's Tale*, *Macbeth*, and *Cymbeline* at the Globe; and, fairly clearly, at home in the country, for the play has elaborate stage directions for other hands to produce it. It was performed on Hallowmas Night, 1 November 1611, at Whitehall 'before the King's Majesty'. It found favour with the public, while Jonson's *Catiline* of that year did not. He wrote, not ill-naturedly but grumpily, in introducing his *Bartholomew Fair*, 'if there be never a servant-monster [Caliban] in the Fair, who can help it, nor a nest of antics [spirits like Ariel]. He [Ben] is loth to make Nature afraid in his plays, like those that beget *Tales, Tempests,* and such-like drolleries.' But the drolleries have proved immortal.

The atmosphere of *The Tempest* is peculiarly one of nostalgia and farewell, and at the end Prospero takes leave of his magic in saying farewell to the enchanted isle. Many have seen in the master's leave-taking Shakespeare's own prospective withdrawal from the practice of his art. With our fuller knowledge of the writer now, and of the way he thought, laying hand upon everything in his experience for his work, it is likely that he had himself in mind, as years earlier he had had with Berowne. 'Our revels now are ended', he says, and:

> these our actors
> As I foretold you, were all spirits and
> Are melted into air, into thin air.
> And, like the baseless fabric of this vision,
> The cloud-capped towers, the gorgeous palaces,
> The solemn temples, the great globe itself –
> Yea, all which it inherit – shall dissolve
> And, like this insubstantial pageant faded,
> Leave not a rack behind.   [*The Tempest*, IV.i.148]

Throughout his work Shakespeare was much given to double-talk, the double-talk of the imagination: there is a secondary suggestion of the Globe here. Perhaps it was he, after all, who had suggested the grandiose name – so like him. Strangely enough, or prophetically, the Globe was in a couple of years to dissolve – by fire, at the performance of his last play, *Henry VIII*.

THAT SHAKESPEARE had had nothing to do with the publication of the *Sonnets* – passed on to Thorpe by Sir William Harvey – we can tell from the fact that he did not read the proofs, as he did with his two long poems. Nor could he ever have published them – as did poets like Spenser, Drayton, Daniel and Constable with their own sonnets – for they are too revealing, too near the bone, and give a damning portrait of the woman with whom he had been for a time infatuated, and not a depiction of himself to be proud of. A couple of years after, there came another reminder of the past: Emilia Lanier put forth a volume of verse – now of the utmost rarity, since only a few incomplete copies have survived – which throws a fascinating, corroborative light upon it.[5]

Her little volume of verse, *Salve Deus Rex Judaeorum*, reveals that she had undergone a religious conversion, very understandable with her temperament and the tribulations she had undergone. She had had plenty in her past to be converted from, though she is still as 'high-minded' as ever – nearly all the poems are addressed to countesses. To Susan, Dowager Countess of Kent, she writes:

> Come, you that were the mistress of my youth,
> The noble guide of my ungoverned days. . . .

Young ladies are adjured now to:

> avoid the bait
> Of worldly pleasures, living always free
> From sword, from violence, and from ill report.

Each of these last she had known from experience: both the old Lord

5 cf. my *Simon Forman: Sex and Society in Shakespeare's Age*, pp. 116–17.

Chamberlain and the man to whom she had been married off, Alfonso Lanier, had fought as soldiers; both Shakespeare and Forman are at one as to her ill reputation, as with regard to everything else about her.

What is so revealing to us is that she prints, along with the poems, a prose defence of women, an aggressive reply to men's defaming of them, only two years after the damning portrait of herself, recognizable if unnamed, which had been published in the *Sonnets*. Shakespeare could never have published them – the only thing to do was to maintain silence. Emilia speaks with bitterness of men, a familiar enough reaction among women sharing her experience of them; but her outburst is unique, unexampled in that age, against 'men, who – forgetting they were born of women, nourished of women and that if it were not by the means of women they would be quite extinguished out of the world and a final end of them all – do, like vipers, deface the wombs wherein they were bred'. And more to the same effect, furious – the same old temperament recognizable, in spite of her conversion.

She was a woman of strong personality, a tough creature, who went on up to 1639, the threshold of the Civil War. She refers back to early favour with Queen Elizabeth, as an orphan of one of her Italian musicians:

> So that I live closed up in sorrow's cell
> Since great Eliza's favour blessed my youth.[6]

This is in keeping with what she had told Forman in 1597; everything we learn about her from Forman and herself is completely consistent with what Shakespeare writes about her, and his experience at her hands. All the same, it is corroborative and adds further conviction that the woman to whom he fell victim was one of exceptional literary, as well as musical, cultivation, an educated person with a knowledge of Renaissance classical terms of reference, again understandable with her Italianate background. Hardly any women wrote verse in England at the time; after Philip Sidney's sister, the Countess of Pembroke, Shakespeare's Dark Lady was the best woman poet.

THE HARD-WORKING PLAYER and playwright could afford to take life easily now: he had achieved the reality, as well as the status, of independent gentleman he had aimed at all along. He is always referred to respectfully as Master Shakespeare. Probably retired from acting, he spent more of his time at Stratford; there are records of his being in residence there at least in September 1611, October 1614, September 1615, and in March and April 1616 to the end. Naturally he would have been there a good deal besides.

He was in London to give evidence in the case concerning the Mountjoys' daughter and son-in-law on 11 May 1612. He is described as 'William Shakespeare of Stratford upon Avon in the county of Warwick, gentleman, of the age of 48 years'. Perfectly correct. He had known the parties to the suit for some ten years, and considered that Bellot was 'a very good and industrious servant'. Mountjoy's wife 'did solicit and *entreat*' him [a favourite word] to effect the same marriage, and he did 'move and persuade' Bellot thereto. He could not remember what portion was promised with the daughter. Daniel Nicholas said that the young couple 'were made sure by Mr Shakespeare, by giving their consent and agreed to marry'. It was hoped to

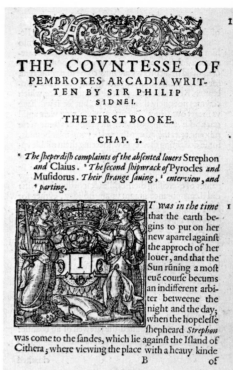

Sidney's *Arcadia*, which much influenced Shakespeare

[6] cf. my *Simon Forman: Sex and Society in Shakespeare's Age*, pp. 116–17.

111

press Shakespeare for more details on 19 June, but there was no further examination; presumably he was back at Stratford.

There his lawyer cousin, Thomas Greene, was town clerk, and lived at New Place for a time in 1609 while waiting to move into his own house. In June 1611 Shakespeare and his cousin both contributed to the cost of promoting a bill in Parliament for the better repair of highways – a public service. In March 1613 he was in London for the purchase of his house in Blackfriars, and next month was designing an emblem or motto for a shield Burbage was painting for the Earl of Rutland. The Earl had been one of Essex's followers and was a friend of Southampton, the circle to which Shakespeare had been affiliated since 1591–2. In November 1614 Thomas Greene was in London reporting 'my cousin Shakespeare coming yesterday to town' with his son-in-law, Dr John Hall; he remained there over Christmas, the chief time for plays at Court.

During the winter of 1612–13 the long negotiations for a Protestant marriage between the Princess Elizabeth and Frederick, Prince Palatine of

Fletcher, who succeeded
Shakespeare as
the Company's dramatist

the Rhine, were at length concluded : the marriage was to take place early the following year. This Princess was an outgoing and popular personality, a god-daughter of the great Queen. Elizabethan memories – not very agreeable to James I – came surging back; Shakespeare, always sensitive to the popular mood, responded yet once more, for the last time, with *Henry VIII*.

With that play the magnificent coil, like a splendid, glittering snake, was really complete. He ended, as he had begun, with an English chronicle play, fulfilling the cycle. We have noticed how, all through, his scheming mind had planned forward. Holinshed, faithful stand-by since the second edition came out in 1587 – on the threshold of Shakespeare's acting and writing career – served again for source; he also read up in Hall's *Chronicle*, Foxe's *Acts and Monuments*, and Cavendish's life of Wolsey. Hence the more favourable rendering of the Cardinal than had come down in either Protestant or Catholic tradition – Shakespeare's own magnanimity is in it too.

The new play was performed, along with five others of Shakespeare's, out of the fourteen given at court for the wedding festivities of Princess Elizabeth. It is from that marriage that Queen Elizabeth II descends. More to our purpose is the reverberation of the name at the time: the dramatist characteristically took his opportunity to pay tribute – at last – to the glories of the age of which he was to become, in time, the chief. Again, it is so typical of his tact that he does not celebrate the triumphs of war – which would not appeal to the unwarlike James – but to the internal concord that Elizabeth I had maintained: he writes in the guise of prophecy:

> In her days every man shall eat in safety
> Under his own vine that he plants, and sing
> The merry songs of peace to all his neighbours.
> [*King Henry VIII*, v.35]

This is the theme that would appeal to her successor, who hoped to go down to history as the monarch who would bring peace to Europe. Alas for such hopes ! – the war raged on in Europe for thirty years, to be succeeded by the civil wars in England, Scotland and Ireland.

Even this play about the past has contemporary references linking it to the time. Here is the new perspective of American colonization opening up – 'Have we some strange Indian with the great tool come to Court, the women so besiege us ? Bless me, what a fry of fornication is at door ! On my Christian conscience, this one christening will beget a thousand.' Here is the familiar bawdy touch of the old master. The christening may have aroused some echoes in the chambers of his mind; for Elizabeth I was the daughter of Henry VIII and Anne Boleyn, whose sister Mary had been Henry's mistress and, when discarded, married off to William Carey. *Their* son was Henry Carey, Lord Chamberlain Hunsdon, whose mistress Emilia. . . .

At a public performance of the play at the Globe, 29 July 1613, the theatre burned down. It seems that *Henry VIII* was produced with pomp and circumstance, and cannon shot off at the King's entry to a masque at the Cardinal's ignited the thatch round the great O. Stage directions were elaborate, evidently for others to produce in the author's absence. The destruction of the theatre – recorded by Ben Jonson in verse – was a considerable loss to the part-owners and sharers of the Fellowship. But so prosperous was the premier company that the Globe was rebuilt finer than before; meanwhile, the King's Men went on tour.

By this time their profits from performances at Court were four times as much as they had received under the careful Elizabeth, with her cousin, the Lord Chamberlain, as their patron. And by this time it was said that they were taking £1000 a winter more at Blackfriars than they had done formerly at the Globe. By the end of James's reign the takings from the much smaller Blackfriars audience were more than twice as much as at the big, popular Globe. The audiences were growing apart – the integration of Elizabethan society itself breaking down – and the King's Men were becoming associated more and more in the public mind with Blackfriars.

This development, so clearly reflected in the last plays of the old master, was carried further by his successor as the Company's dramatist-in-chief, John Fletcher. Fletcher and his friend Beaumont had written their first pieces, *The Knight of the Burning Pestle* and *The Faithful Shepherdess*, for the earlier Blackfriars, where they had had little success. Now, with Blackfriars under the new management of the most experienced company in London, they had a great hit with *Philaster*. This settled Fletcher's future for him; Beaumont died early, though his name was continued in later publication. Year by year Fletcher poured out his plays, more prolifically than the master he admired, for he had not the double burden of acting as well as writing.

It seems that Shakespeare lent a hand to his disciple, who succeeded him, for some touches for *The Two Noble Kinsmen*. Probably enough; what is more noteworthy is the fascination Shakespeare's work exercised upon Fletcher's mind: he seems to have thought it a good recipe for success, often simply to reverse the situation in one of Shakespeare's plays, giving it a new twist or changing the sexes. *Philaster* seems to have taken *Hamlet* for its point of departure (as *Rosencrantz and Guildenstern* in our time, such is the creative power of Shakespeare's genius in suitable soil, such as Keats for instance, or Scott, or Tennyson). *The Woman's Prize* reverses *The Taming of the Shrew*; *The Custom of the Country* offers a variation on *Measure for Measure*. Echoes of Shakespeare appear in practically all of the enormous output of his successor. Even so, it was only one side of the Elizabethan's mind that

Shakespeare's son-in-law,
Dr Hall, prescribes for Drayton

OBSERV. XXII.

MR. *Drayton*, an excellent Poet, labouring of a Tertian, was cured by the following: R *the Emetick Infusion* ℥i. *Syrup of Violets a spoonful*: *mix them.* This given, wrought very well both upwards and downwards.

Æ: SVÆ. 30.   A.D. 1599.

Drayton, poet-laureate,
Shakespeare's fellow-
Warwickshire man

appealed to and inspired the Jacobean. The universality of that mind reflected the integration of an heroic age; everything in that age is expressed by Shakespeare, except its religious nonsense. And that led shortly to the outbreak of the Civil War.

AT STRATFORD life proceeded quietly and kindly. Shakespeare had had the intelligent companionship of his doctor son-in-law from 1607 when he married Susanna; Susanna took after her father, 'witty above her sex ... something of Shakespeare was in that': (witty then meant intelligent). Their only child, called Elizabeth – we should note that, for it does not appear to be a family name – was born in 1608. He had also the companionship in summer at Clifford Chambers of the poet Drayton, whom Dr Hall treated for tertian ague (malaria). In 1612 his brother Gilbert died, in 1613 his brother Richard.

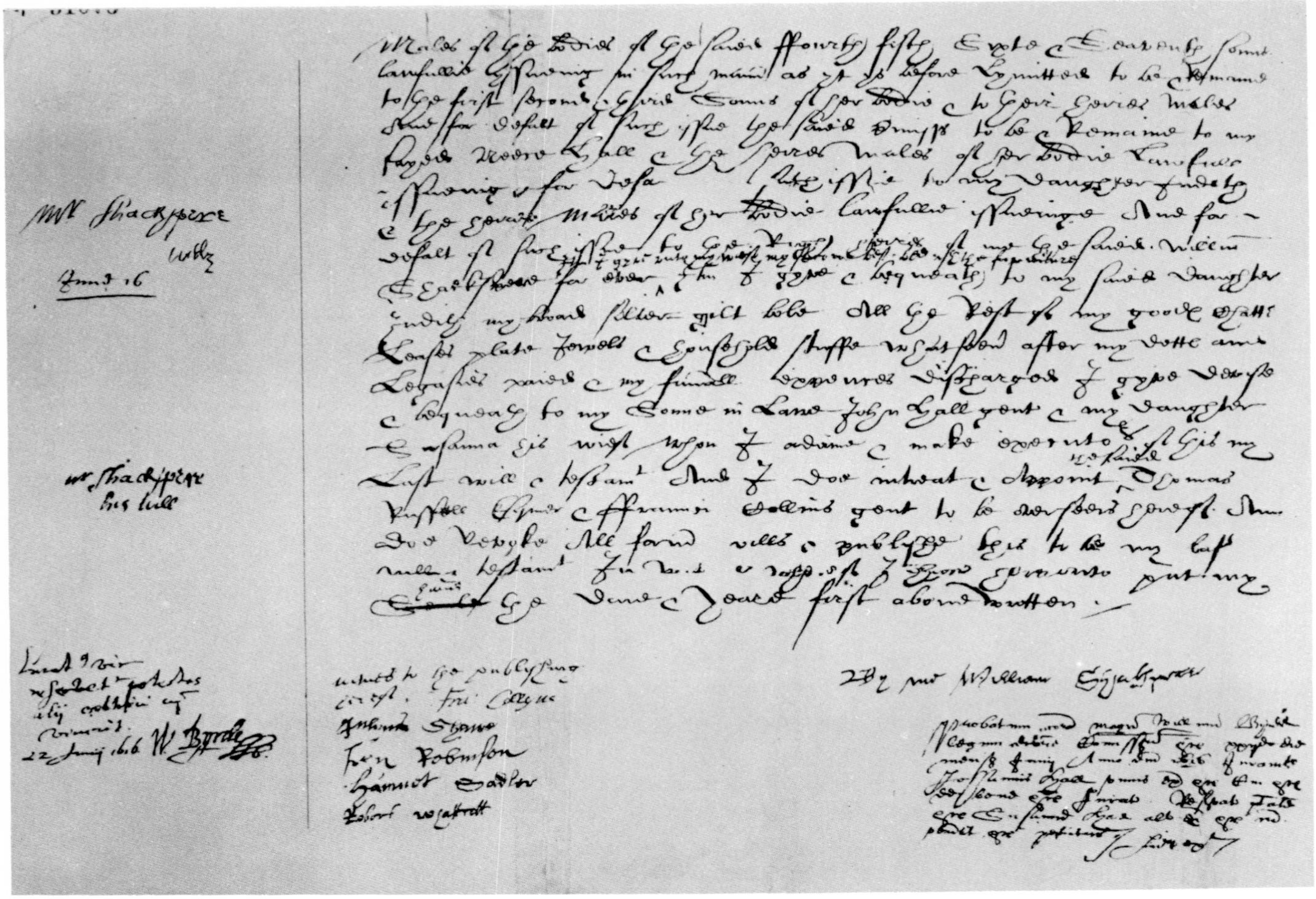

Mr Shackspere
wills
Anno 16

wr shackspere
his will

Shakespeare's will is proved

That summer Susanna brought suit for defamation against an ungentlemanly young gentleman, John Lane, out along the meadows at Alvescot. He had said that she had 'the running of the reins, and had been naught with Ralph Smith'. We now realize that 'the running of the reins' meant venereal trouble; nothing improbable in that for an Elizabethan: her father had sought remedy for love's distemper at Bath much earlier.

Next year, 1614, Stratford was devastated by fire as once before, and yet again the fortunate family escaped, with no damage to their property. Out at Welcombe there was trouble over enclosures, which might have somewhat affected the value of Shakespeare's tithes. He did not appear to think so, though cousin Greene was concerned for his interests. In February 1616 a husband was found for Shakespeare's unintelligent daughter, Judith, though not a very good one. Judith couldn't write – ordinary people often could not in that age: literacy was for the intelligent. The husband-to-be was Thomas Quiney, son of Shakespeare's well-educated friend, Richard Quiney, who had been bailiff of the borough, like Shakespeare's father. Thomas, however, was not much of it; a vintner, he drank and had himself been before the court for giving a girl an illegitimate child. Shakespeare's will showed doubts of him, but he provided sufficiently for Judith. Their children did not live.

Shakespeare made his will on Lady Day, 25 March 1616, 'in perfect health and memory, God be praised'. It is a very characteristic document, generous and neighbourly; he seems to have thought of everybody. The details are well known; we need not go into them all, merely note a few significant items.

Susanna was his heir, and she got the bulk of the property, real and personal. She would take care of her mother, but there was the kindly specification of the second best bed for her – probably the one she was accustomed to. To his sister Joan Hart he left the old house in Henley Street for her life, with £20, all his clothes and £5 each for her three sons. There was a generous bequest of £10 to the poor of the parish, and a number of neighbours were remembered: his sword to go to Thomas Combe of the college by the church; money for mourning rings to his old friend Hamnet Sadler, godfather of his dead boy, neighbour Reynolds (a Catholic), Anthony and John Nash, gentlemen; and 'to my Fellows, John Heming, Richard Burbage, and Henry Condell'.

His will recited the regular Protestant formula, 'I commend my soul into the hands of God my Creator, hoping and assured by believing through the only merits of Jesus Christ, my Saviour, to be made partaker of life everlasting.' He died, as he had lived, an ordinary conforming member of the Church of England. He was not a Marlowe, or a Ben Jonson, bent on being different from ordinary humanity.

When he made his will in March he was in good health. In April he contracted a sudden fever – rumour in Stratford said, later, after a too merry meeting with Drayton and Ben Jonson. On St George's Day, 23 April 1616, he died, and was buried – after the exceptionally short interval of only two days (did Dr Hall diagnose an infectious fever?) – in the church where he and all his family had been baptized. There, in the following years, his immediate family were gathered around him, in the chancel where the gentry of a parish were usually buried.

❧ *Epilogue* ❧

SHAKESPEARE'S WIDOW, Anne Hathaway, though over eight years older, survived him by seven years. He was fifty-two when he died; she died in 1623 and 'did earnestly desire to be laid in the same grave with him', an old sexton said, but no-one durst touch his gravestone for fear of the curse inscribed in his lines thereon. It certainly is a curious – and may, for all I know, be a unique – feature; for once, let us transcribe it in the antique spelling:

> God Frend for Jesus sake forbeare,
> To digg the dust encloased heare!
> Bleste be ye man yt spares thes stones,
> And curst be he yt moves my bones.

The warning seems to have held people off.

In the same year his Fellows in the Company, led by Heming and Condell, paid him the exceptional tribute of collecting his plays, which were the property of the Company, and publishing them in what is so famous as the First Folio. It was not at all usual to do this – only Ben Jonson had had the hardihood to collect his – and now he was called in to help with the heavy undertaking. He contributed the long biographical poem which places Shakespeare – so generously then, so justly in the eyes of posterity – with Aeschylus, Sophocles, Euripides. (I agree with Dryden in holding him their superior.) Others, too, paid tribute, from Oxford and Cambridge. We know that *Hamlet*, and possibly others of his plays, were presented at both universities. Now there spoke up for Cambridge Hugh Holland, who had been schooled, like Ben, under Camden at Westminster; for Oxford, Leonard Digges and James Mabbe, friend of Florio. Shortly, the name in our literature second only to Shakespeare, John Milton, would pay tribute, in 1630:

1616

Marc(h)

1 A Infant of ...
2 ...
3 Katheren ...
5 Joan ...
5 ... fillia ...
9 margret fillia ...
15 margret wheeler & her child

Aprill
3 Thomas dixon
5 margret fillia John James
9 sons twines of Rich bushman
15 will navie gent
16 A Infant of the woodward
17 will hartt haller   ✗
21 Elizabeth fillia will beamish
23 Ane corke widow
24 Richard pynder
25 will Shakspere gent   ✗

may
9 margret fillia Robert ...
11 sons twines of will ...
23 Thomas bramley de drayton
25 Thomas bradshew ...

1 Alce hearinge widow
7 Ane corke widow
14 Elizabeth cuninge...
19 Alce fillia Roger mollener
21 A Infant of Robert ward
26 Roger mollener
26 Thomas fillius henery pratt
30 Thomas fillius ... servitor

Dear son of memory, great heir of Fame. . . .
Thou in our wonder and astonishment
Hast built thyself a livelong monument.[1]

The theatrical origin of this big undertaking was emphasized by Heming and Condell ascribing it 'only to keep the memory of so worthy a friend and Fellow as was our Shakespeare'. They could have wished that 'the author himself had lived to have set forth and overseen his own writings'. But, as we have seen, he had died rather unexpectedly, and it had been no easy job to bring together all his plays, from the prompt-books and such manuscripts as the Company possessed, the imperfect and surreptitious quartos, some of which had been corrected by better, emended issues. Altogether they collected thirty-six plays, half of which might have been lost without them. They knew better than anyone – except Jonson – the ease and rapidity with which he had written: 'his mind and hand went together, and what he thought he uttered with . . . easiness'.

They were plays which, whatever critics might say, had already withstood the criticism that mattered: those who set themselves up for judges 'and sit on the stage at Blackfriars, or the Cockpit, to arraign plays daily – know, these plays have had their trial already and stood out all appeals'. That was the test these actors considered important; they appended a list of those who had acted in them and with whom Shakespeare had acted. Here are the names of those who had won such renown for the Elizabethan drama – a roll-call as grand as that of the voyagers, the Elizabethan seamen, the brilliant throng around the Queen, her Court and government, or the poets, prose writers, composers. Shakespeare himself is followed by Burbage, Heming, Augustine Phillips, Will Kemp, Pope, Bryan, Condell; other familiars are Will Sly, Cowley, Robert Armin, and handsome Nathan Field (himself playwright as well as player), with John Underwood and William Ostler, who had been boy actors before becoming King's Men. The big volume was very properly dedicated to the brothers Pembroke, Lord Chamberlain, and Montgomery, who was to succeed him. Pembroke was for years a close acquaintance of Burbage and devoted to him.

Stratford-upon-Avon was already distinguished – so the historian, Sir William Dugdale, tells us – in that 'it gave birth and sepulture to our late famous poet, William Shakespeare'. There Susanna, her husband and daughter Elizabeth held on together at New Place. At eighteen a husband was found for Elizabeth in Thomas Nash, aged thirty-three, a son of friend John Nash to whom her father had left money for a mourning ring. In 1635 Dr Hall died; as a widow Susanna had the sad privilege of receiving Charles I's Queen at New Place in 1643, in the confusion and break-up of the Civil War. The sympathies of the town were with Parliament; it was to be expected that those of Shakespeare's family would be with the King.

On the death of her husband, Elizabeth married a Northamptonshire gentleman, John Barnard, and left Stratford for their house in the country at Abington, near Northampton. At the Restoration he was knighted; so Shakespeare's only grandchild became a lady of title, Lady Barnard of Abington. When she died in 1670 she left money to her poor relations, the

[1] John Milton, 'On Shakespeare', first published as prefatory verses to the Second Folio, 1632.

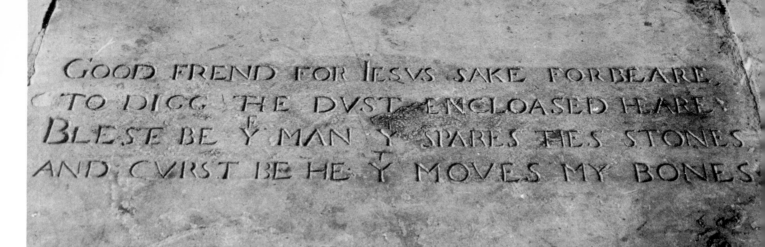

GOOD FREND FOR IESVS SAKE FORBEARE,
TO DIGG THE DVST ENCLOASED HEARE
BLESE BE Y MAN Y SPARES TES STONES
AND CVRST BE HE Y MOVES MY BONES.

Hathaways, back at Stratford; and the two houses in Henley Street, one of them Shakespeare's birth-place, to his great-nephews, Thomas and George Hart. When Sir John Barnard died four years later he mentioned in his will a study of books, and old goods and lumber at Stratford of not much worth, to be destroyed.

Judith's children died young – one of them, Shakespeare Quiney, an attempt to continue the name in vain. His granddaughter, Elizabeth, had no children: with her his direct line died out in only the third generation. But the children of his imagination are alive all over the world.

The verse inscribed on Shakespeare's grave

Acknowledgments

ILLUSTRATIONS in this book are supplied or reproduced by kind permission of the following:

2 Frontispiece based on that in the First Folio of Shakespeare's plays: British Museum, London

8 (above) Shakespeare's home in Henley Street, photographed before it was restored: Shakespeare Birthplace Trust, Stratford

8 (below) Shakespeare's birthplace: British Tourist Authority, London

10 Baptismal font: Radio Times Hulton Picture Library, London

11 (above) Stratford Grammar School, interior: Shakespeare Birthplace Trust, Stratford

11 (below) School scene *c.* 1600: Radio Times Hulton Picture Library, London

12 Charlecote: Edwin Smith

13 The Hare, to the Hunter: John Freeman, London

17 *Venus and Adonis* dedicated to Southampton: Bodleian Library, Oxford

19 *Titus Andronicus*, drawing by Henry Peacham *c.* 1594; first illustration of a Shakespearean production: The Courtauld Institute of Art, London

20 A miniature of Southampton by Nicholas Hilliard: Fitzwilliam Museum, Cambridge

21 Queen Elizabeth I from George Turberville's *The Book of Hunting,* 1573: Mansell Collection, London

22 Lord Burghley, attributed to Arnold van Bronckhorst, *c.* 1560–70: National Portrait Gallery, London

23 Mary, Countess of Southampton: by kind permission of the Duke of Portland

26 Title page, first edition of Shakespeare's *Sonnets*: John Freeman, London

28 Simon Forman visits Emilia Lanier; ms. Ashm. 354, fol. 254R: Bodleian Library, Oxford

30 The plague in London, ms. Ashley 617, title page: British Museum, London

31 (right) Title page from the 1604 edition of Marlowe's *Faustus*, ms. Malone 233 (3) T.P: Bodleian Library, Oxford

31 (left) Title page from the 1624 edition of Marlowe's *Faustus*: John Freeman, London

33 Anne Hathaway's cottage: British Tourist Authority, London

34 Sir Thomas Heneage: Lord Petre, Essex County Council

35 Lord Chamberlain Hunsdon: L. G. Stopford Sackville, Esq.; National Portrait Gallery, London

36–7 (above) London *c.* 1550: Cooper Bridgeman Library, London

36–7 (below) Visscher's map of London: British Museum, London

38 Emilia Lanier consults Simon Forman: Bodleian Library, Oxford

40 Southampton: by kind permission of the Duke of Buccleuch and Queensberry

42 Title page, *A Midsummer Night's Dream*, 1600: Mansell Collection, London

43 The actors in Shakespeare's plays: Shakespeare Birthplace Trust, Stratford

44 (left) William Sly; (right) Edward Alleyn: by kind permission of the Governors, Dulwich College Picture Gallery, London

Acknowledgments

45 Nathan Field: by kind permission of the Governors, Dulwich College Picture Gallery, London
46 Richard Burbage: by kind permission of the Governors, Dulwich College Picture Gallery, London
49 Title page, *The Merchant of Venice*: Radio Times Hulton Picture Library, London
50 Henry Danvers, Earl of Danby: the Woburn Abbey Collection by kind permission of the Marquess of Tavistock and Trustees of the Bedford Estates
52 Shakespeare's Southwark: British Museum, London
55 Title page, first edition of Holinshed's *Chronicles*: John Freeman, London
56 Richard Tarleton: British Museum, London
59 Title page of Armin's play: British Museum, London
61 Shakespeare's coat-of-arms: Shakespeare Birthplace Trust, Stratford
63 Shakespeare's home at New Place: Shakespeare Birthplace Trust, Stratford
64 Guild Chapel: Edwin Smith
66 Ben Jonson, after Abraham Blyenberch: National Portrait Gallery, London
67 Title page of Jonson's play: Bodleian Library, Oxford
68 Queen Elizabeth I in the Garter Procession; from Marcus Gheeraerts's *Proceeding of the Sovereign and Knights Companions of the Order of the Garter and St George's Feast in 1578*: British Museum, London
71 Elizabeth Vernon, Countess of Southampton: National Gallery of Scotland, Edinburgh
72 Robert, 2nd Earl of Essex, by Marcus Gheeraerts the Younger: the Woburn Abbey Collection, by kind permission of the Marquess of Tavistock and Trustees of the Bedford Estates
73 *Richard II,* title-page of Quarto: Radio Times Hulton Picture Library, London
75 Interior of an Elizabethan theatre, The Swan: Mansell Collection, London
75 The Globe
76 Title page, Plutarch's *Lives*: John Freeman, London
78 Francis, Earl of Rutland: Mansell Collection, London
80 *Hamlet*, title-page: British Museum, London
84 Silver Street from Agas's map of London: The Guildhall Library, London
87 List of Court performances, including Shakespeare's plays: Mansell Collection, London
89 Elizabeth I on the title-page of Saxton's *Atlas of England & Wales*, 1579: British Library, London
90 (left) James I by D. Mytens, 1621: National Portrait Gallery, London
90 (right) Anne of Denmark: by gracious permission of Her Majesty the Queen
91 Whitehall Palace, by Wyngaerde: Ashmolean Museum, Oxford
92 A view of The Globe, after Visscher: Rainbird Publishing Group, London
93 Portrait of Shakespeare, artist unknown: National Portrait Gallery, London
94 Two Scottish generals meet the three witches; illustration from an account of Macbeth in Holinshed's *Chronicles*: John Freeman, London

95 Title page, *King Lear*: Bodleian Library, Oxford
96 Shakespeare's Memorial in Holy Trinity Church, Stratford: British Tourist Authority, London
98 The Gunpowder Plot: British Museum, London
102 Holy Trinity Church, Stratford: British Tourist Authority, London
104 The arrival of the English in Virginia: John Freeman, London
107 Simon Forman's account of *Cymbeline*, ms. Ashm. 208, f.206R: Bodleian Library, Oxford
111 From Sidney's *Arcadia*: John Freeman, London
112 John Fletcher, artist unknown: National Portrait Gallery, London
114 Dr Hall's prescription for Drayton: Shakespeare Birthplace Trust, Stratford
115 Michael Drayton, artist unknown: National Portrait Gallery, London
116 Shakespeare's will: Radio Times Hulton Picture Library, London
119 Record of Shakespeare's burial: Shakespeare Birthplace Trust, Stratford
121 Inscription on Shakespeare's grave: Shakespeare Birthplace Trust, Stratford

Picture research by Debbie Beevor

Index

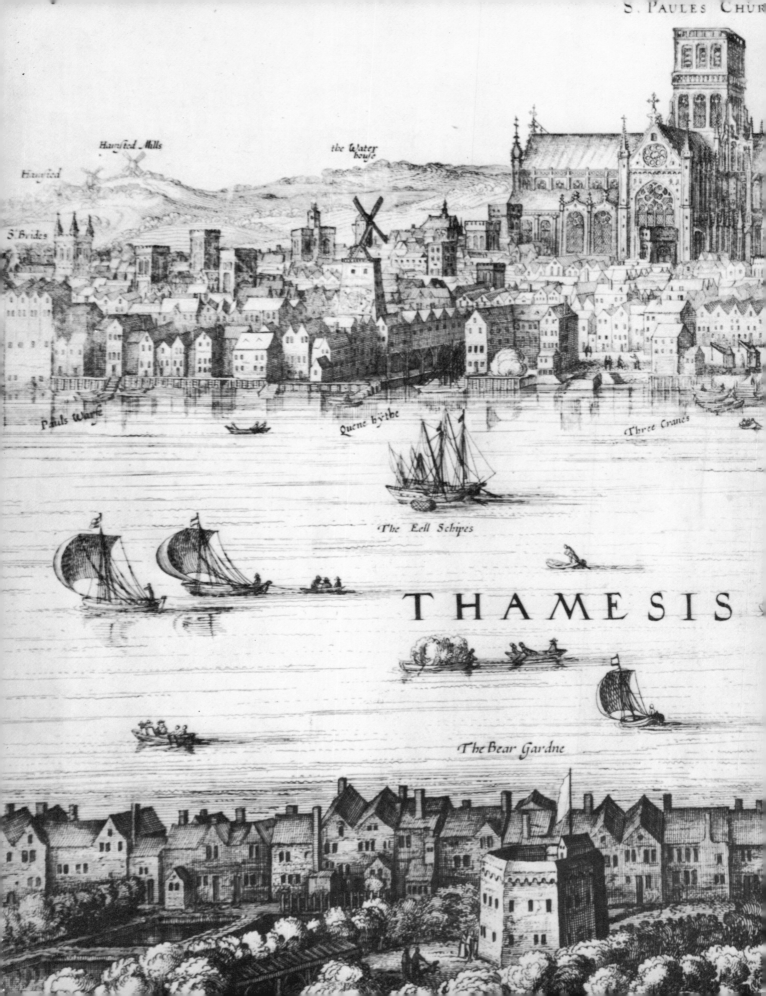